LIVE LIKE A LOCAL IN LOJA: AN EXPAT EXPERIENCE IN ECUADOR

Lily Ann Fouts

Live Like a Local in Loja - Lily Ann Fouts

Copyright © 2017 Lily Ann Fouts

All rights reserved. No part of this book may be used or reproduced in any manner whatsoever without written permission except in the case of brief quotations.

For more information, contact Lily Fouts - lily@lilyannfouts.com.

Dedicated to my dear husband, Keith Fouts.
Your support means the world to me.
I love you!

Table of Contents

Treasure Between Cuenca and Vilcabamba	12
Growing Up in Latin America	18
Getting to Know Loja	26
First Things First: Learn Spanish!	38
Nine Steps to Speaking Spanish	48
Arriving and Finding Your Way Around	69
City Buses and Neighborhoods of Loja	78
The Fun Side of Loja: Art and Culture	101
The Fun Side of Loja: Nature	113
Eating and Shopping	130
Setting Up House	150
Making Friends	173
Culture Clashes	180
Vilcabamba	190
Cuenca	198
Other Towns Near Loja	204
Let the Adventure Begin!	220
Bonus: My Next Book!	225
Acknowledgments	241

Introduction

"A foreigner had just moved into an apartment I was managing. He actually spoke some Spanish, so I started explaining to him, in Spanish, how to work the lock on the door." My husband Keith and I were in Vilcabamba for the day, listening to our friend at a restaurant in the plaza. After almost three years away, we had returned to Ecuador and were catching up with all the friends we had made in 2014. Maria, a local from the town, leaned toward us over the table, telling her story in a soft voice so nobody around could hear.

"All of a sudden, the man blew up at me," Maria continued. "He said, 'Why are you speaking to me in Spanish? You speak good English. Show some respect and speak to me in my own language!' He was actually shouting at me!" Maria paused, a look of pain on her face as she remembered the shock of the moment.

"I apologized and switched to English, but inside I was so upset. I wanted to tell him, 'We are in Ecuador!'"

Maria stopped and looked around to make sure nobody was listening, then leaned in again, continuing even more quietly, "So many of the foreigners who move here expect everything to be the same as it was in their country, but it isn't. Things aren't so easy here. A lot of them don't even try to learn Spanish. They expect everyone to talk to them in English."

Why do people close themselves off from other cultures and only associate with their own? What's the point of moving out of your country if you have interest in socializing only with your own countrymen in a "Little Canada" or "Little America" abroad? Personally, I find it deeply tragic, and as a North American in Ecuador I was embarrassed by the behavior I observed in some of the expatriates.

Expats choose to move abroad for many different reasons. I think most have some interest in the culture of the country they choose to adopt as their new home. Most, too, want to be accepted and embraced by the locals in their new neighborhoods.

When too many expats move into the same area, however, it begins to lose the local flavor that so enchanted the first expats who moved there. As more and more expats arrive, they tend to cluster into a tight-knit community, creating—though unintentional—an "us-versus-them" feeling with the locals. I noticed a definite rift between the locals and the expats in Vilcabamba. There seems to be a general distrust of each other. Sadly, some expats are making a bad name for foreigners and the locals are becoming more wary. I see the frustration in their faces as they attempt to communicate and do business with expats who won't learn the basics of their language. Maria and other locals told me stories of expats who became angry with them because they didn't speak English. Other stories emerged of alcohol and drug abuse among the expats.

During each of our trips to Ecuador, I spoke with many people about their observations and feelings about foreigners. When so many expats flood an area that the language of business shifts to that of the expats, the locals feel an understandable sense of resentment. Add in the "gringo economy"—where prices of food, housing and everything else rise to higher levels as expats conduct business and attempt to earn money off of each other—and soon the locals find it increasingly difficult to afford life in their own town anymore. Expats and tourists—especially those who parade their wealth—then become targets for crime.

Most of those I spoke to were apprehensive about the influx of foreigners, who too often come with an attitude much like an expat I overheard in Vilcabamba, telling a tourist, "The thing I really like about living here is that I don't have to learn Spanish. You can easily do everything in English here."

"Visit us," is the general consensus among the locals, "but don't stay unless you are willing to live like us and learn our language and culture."

It's easy to see why Vilcabamba is such an attractive destination—especially for those who like smaller towns, healthy living, and enjoy living off the land. It is a paradise with near-perfect weather and beautiful surroundings. However, the expat-to-local population ratio is well beyond the tipping point, with the largest per-capita concentration of foreigners in the entire country. Estimates on the ratio of expats to locals in the town varies, but some sources estimate foreigners in Vilcabamba account for 80% of the town's economy.

There are probably some neighborhoods in Cuenca and several other towns in Ecuador facing similar fates. What can be done about it? I believe the answer is to think carefully about how our presence as foreigners might impact the place to which we are moving. Just as many people in the U.S. might resent an influx of Mexicans who refuse to learn the English language or the American culture and want all their services provided in Spanish, so Ecuadorians resent large populations of foreigners who drive up the cost of living, refuse to speak Spanish and do not respect their way of life.

Does this mean that none of the expats in Vilcabamba or Cuenca have made great local friends? Does it mean nobody has done a good job of mingling with the local community? Of course not! We met one man who had made many local friends and was greeted cordially by everyone he encountered—and I have heard stories of many others. However, the uncharacteristically cold attitude of several of the locals toward us betrayed the negative experiences they had endured with other foreigners, and they were tired of it.

Fortunately, there is a solution to these problems. There are still plenty of places in Ecuador that are relatively untouched by foreign residents. In order to maximize a positive relationship with the Ecuadorians, I recommend finding a town or neighborhood that has the characteristics you love—but a very small number of expats. Learn Spanish as quickly as you can and actively work to integrate yourself into the local culture and community in a spirit of respect and openness. Impossible? No.

Hugely challenging? Yes. But those who pull it off successfully will open a door into a world of wonder that they could never have imagined before.

The city we chose was Loja, a beautiful town of just over 180,000 people nestled in the Cuxibamba Valley, at just under 7,000 feet of elevation in the Andes mountains. When we first went to Loja in 2014, I couldn't find much information about it at all! The few general articles that I found talked about how Loja had very few expats, warmer weather than Cuenca, and was the cultural capital of Ecuador. All of these things sounded very good, but I wanted some more practical details about the city. We would just have to figure it out when we got there.

Now that we have had the privilege of living in Loja (twice!) and making new friends there, I have written the book that answers all the questions I had before we went, such as:
- How will we find a place to live?
- What's the city bus system like, and will it be easy to find our way around?
- How safe is it?
- Is the Internet going to be dependable enough for me to get my work done?
- How cold or hot or humid will it feel?
- Will it be hard to make new friends?
- What can we do for fun around Loja?
- What are the neighborhoods like, and where are the best and worst parts of town?

In the second edition of the book, I have

updated information based on the changes over the past three years since our first visit. I've told more stories, corrected some mistakes and typos, added Celsius to the temperatures, expanded chapters and added some new chapters! I added a whole new section on the Loja city bus system, more detailed tourist information, and new stores and resources that did not exist or that I had not been aware of when I first wrote this book. I also wrote more information with the casual traveler in mind—someone who may not be interested in going to Loja long-term, but who would love to visit. For such a traveler, the information on setting up a home in Ecuador may not be relevant, but I hope the information about the area, the cultural insights, and tips for learning some Spanish (though not as necessary if you are just visiting) will be helpful.

These days, it's hard to keep up with all the changes in Ecuador. Since the year 2000, there has been a tremendous amount of development in the country. Loja is changing quickly, too. More and more local businesses are changing the way they operate, putting up websites and Facebook pages, and modernizing. In fact, things have been changing so quickly in recent years that I have also created a bonus companion website to this book. Continue reading to learn how to access it!

The companion site includes more up-to-date information and links to useful resources in Loja, and when you sign up for access, I'll send you some additional bonuses, including copies of several of my interviews with locals and expats in Loja! I hope that this book and its companion site will help you to formulate a clearer idea of whether you would enjoy living in Loja for any length of time, and also serve as a guide for you if you do choose to spend some time there. Watch for instructions on accessing this bonus content further on in the book!

In Loja, we found overwhelmingly friendly and generous residents, interesting new foods, a pleasant climate and beautiful scenery. Nevertheless, it does have its faults, and it does not appeal to everyone. Those who have trouble adapting to new cultures may find it very difficult to live in Loja.

If you wish to adopt Loja (or any place in Latin America) as your new home, I advocate making an attempt to at least learn the basics of Spanish and integrating with the local culture as quickly as possible. It's perfectly fine to socialize with fellow expats, but if you wish to associate *exclusively* with people who speak your mother tongue, then find a country that speaks your language.

After reading that last paragraph you may be offended and tempted to throw this book in the garbage if language seems like a major obstacle to you. But wait! Learning Spanish is not as hard as it might seem. Even if you think you're bad at languages or you've tried before and felt like a failure, take heart. Read Chapter Four on learning Spanish and try some of the tips and tricks I share there. Learning another language is not as hard as most people think it is. Most people just go about it the wrong way.

In this book, I'll help you explore Loja as a place to explore for fun as well as a potential place to move to for those who are interested in living within the Ecuadorian culture. I'll also help you discover ways to quickly learn Spanish, meet local people, and make friends. While much of the information here will be specific to Loja, I hope that you will also find the principles valuable for integration in any other part of Ecuador or Latin America, should you want to move or travel long-term there.

My goal for you is that by the end of this book, you'll have a clear idea of whether or not Loja could be a good fit for you, and how you could integrate yourself into the local culture in Loja or any other part of Latin America.

If after reading this book you think Loja seems to hold a lot of potential for your personal likes and tastes, I encourage you to spend a few weeks or months there, get to know some people and get a feel for living in the town before making a permanent commitment. I will show you how to do that, too!

Ecuador can be a great place to live—and Loja might be a good option for you, depending on your tastes. Those who make an effort to learn and respect its ways are generally welcomed with open arms, and that is a wonderful feeling! This was our experience. I'm excited to present this region to you—its pros and cons—and help you learn whether this could be an option for you. Let's dive in!

CHAPTER ONE

The Treasure Between Cuenca and Vilcabamba

Ecuador has morphed from a struggling developing country to an increasingly modern one, with a stable government, good infrastructure, any climate a person could want (simply pick an elevation with the temperature you like!), and a relatively low crime rate—especially compared to Central America.

Cuenca claims fame as the most popular retirement city in Ecuador. It's a beautiful UNESCO World Heritage city with gorgeous churches, wonderful museums, frequent cultural events, spring-like weather, safe drinking water and modern shopping centers. North Americans and Europeans live a comfortable life on much less than they would spend on a similar standard of living back home. As a result, thousands of expats have flocked to Cuenca, often congregating together in "gringo" neighborhoods and socializing primarily with other expats.

Generally gracious people, the Ecuadorian nationals have mixed feelings toward the foreigners who come to live in their land—particularly those who refuse to get to know their language and culture. The temptation to raise the prices and earn more money from this influx of wealth is understandably great, but it also then causes problems for their own people as prices rise to the level that locals struggle to afford.

Expats who refuse to integrate into the local culture do a disservice not only to the locals, but to themselves. They are more often over-charged by merchants, targeted by beggars and thieves, and generally resented by the locals. It behooves future expats to take an honest and responsible look at how their presence in their adopted country could affect the locals who live there.

My background makes me unusually sensitive to the cultural rifts I see happening in some parts of Ecuador. I lived in Mexico as a child, between the ages of eight and thirteen. We lived in an average middle class Mexican neighborhood and all of our friends were locals. We played, worked, shopped and lived our life alongside them and they treated us like family.

Occasionally we met American or European tourists, and many of our interactions with them were pleasant and fun. Sometimes we offered to show them around, acting as their guides and interpreters for the area. Most of them were respectful and appreciative.

Sometimes, however, we saw tourists complaining about everything and acting as though they were superior to the people who lived there. A few foreigners even chose to live in the area, but some would cluster together and interact with the locals as little as possible, treating the ones they did meet as though they were servants. People like that embarrassed me. I remember being almost in tears after observing one particularly condescending foreigner interacting with a local, and just wishing I could be Mexican like everyone else so nobody would think I was like that rude person.

As an adult, I have traveled to many parts of the world —including several Latin American countries—and observed over and over again the different attitudes of travelers and expats toward the locals. The travelers who make an effort to learn even a few words of the local language, interact with the locals, and treat them with full respect always come away with a new insight, more appreciation and amazing stories.

Having grown up as an expat in a Latin American country (a story I will share in more detail in the next chapter) and traveled to various countries around the world, I came to Ecuador with a different perspective than many other foreigners, and in this book I hope to share that perspective along with some practical and valuable information for successful living in Loja.

I have the distinct impression that Cuenca—like Vilcabamba—may be reaching a tipping point, at least in certain parts of the city. It's time for expats to make more of an effort to learn the Ecuadorian way of life. Perhaps it's even time to look at other less "foreigner-infested" towns where integration with the locals can happen more naturally.

For those who enjoy mountains, spring-like weather, birds, music, and a wide range of interesting places to visit within a half-day drive, Loja is worthy of consideration. Located just over 200 winding highway kilometers south of Cuenca and 45 kilometers north of Vilcabamba, Loja is home to two major Ecuadorian universities—as well as other university branch campuses—and a school of music that has produced some of the country's best musicians.

Thanks to its latitude and elevation, the weather in Loja is never extreme, and usually hovers in the 60s and 70s Fahrenheit (around 15 to 26 Celsius) during the day and the 40s and 50s (7 to 12 Celsius) at night, year round. A rain jacket and/or umbrella and a light jacket are usually all that you'll need for staying comfortable in town. The climate experiences a relative humidity of around 75%, a major rainy season around February to April and a smaller rainy season in October. Due to its location in the mountains the weather is unpredictable, but even in the rainy season the sun often appears for at least a little while each day. While the weather never goes below 40° (4.5 Celsius) even at night, there is a short cold season that hits around June and July where people tend to bundle up in warmer clothing. If you are in Loja during this time of year, you will notice that the unheated and uninsulated buildings are much colder than what you're used to in North America or Europe, so bring some extra base layers (fleece, wool, etc.)!

For lovers of nature and the great outdoors, Loja offers many hiking and birdwatching opportunities in its city parks, surrounding hillsides, and nearby Podocarpus

National Park—one of the most bio-diverse parks in the world.

Unlike the locals in Cuenca and Vilcabamba, natives of Loja have not yet developed a strong attitude or opinion of the few foreigners within the city. They do, however, have a fear that their city could someday become like Cuenca or Vilcabamba. Stories and rumors abound.

In our experience, when we made an effort to interact with the locals, spoke to them in their own language, and expressed an interest in their way of life, they accepted us wholeheartedly and were actually sad to see us go. They treated us fairly—even generously—in the markets, charging us the same prices as the locals. Almost never did anyone ask us for money; beggars and homeless people are rare in Loja (though we noticed more in 2017, reportedly migrants from the coastal area since the devastating earthquake in 2016).

When I asked them about their feelings toward foreigners in general, the locals in Loja were mostly open and frank with me. I sensed a mixture of curiosity, admiration, and apprehension toward expats. I had the feeling that any expat who would take the time to learn their language and respect them would be heartily welcomed into the community. As foreigners, we will never become fully like a native—we will always be considered "different"—but we can absolutely develop deep friendships, be loved and respected, and live like a local.

My dream for anyone who chooses Loja as their new home is that they would learn to love and appreciate the local culture for what it is—and it will not always be as smooth as life back home. The cultural differences will take time to get used to, and there may be periods of intense frustration. But in the world of expats, I believe there will be winners and there will be losers.

The losers will refuse to fully love and enjoy the country they have adopted. They will complain about the inefficiencies and the inconveniences. They will not learn the language. They will not trust the locals, and the locals will not trust them. In this "us-vs.-them" world, there will gradually be an increase in prices, and an increase in crime. A downward spiral of fear, resentment and hate will follow. It's already happening in some areas.

The winners, in contrast, will learn Spanish and take an interest in their new community. They will seek out activities and events where they can form relationships with locals and learn more about their way of life. As they take a genuine interest in their adopted town, the locals will feel respected and treat the newcomers with fairness and respect in return. The newcomers will be invited into the homes of the locals and treated with love and generosity. Sure, there will be some who may try to take advantage of these foreigners, but others will step in and protect them. They will let them know if they are being over-charged for something or if they need to be careful in certain areas. The winners will be embraced as a part of the community and, if they ever leave, the community will mourn their departure.

If you're ready to be a winner, keep reading. In addition to learning all about Loja, I hope you'll also find some golden principles that you can take with you and learn to live like a local in any community you choose to move to—whether that's Loja or some other place. Get ready to win!

CHAPTER TWO

Growing Up in Latin America

People often ask me why I lived in Mexico as a child. The short answer to that question is that my sister and I had been kidnapped and our abductor took us down there to hide us.

My abductor—also known as my non-custodial mother—actually had a good reason for what she was doing, though she was brave to do it. Through a series of lies and trickery, our abusive father had gained custody of my sister and me in an ugly court battle. My mom, unable to convince the courts to reverse their decision, took us during our summer visit and we became fugitives.

We started out bouncing around in the South—Mississippi, Tennessee, Oklahoma—but then we went to Mexico. It's a long story that I don't have the time to get into in this little book about Loja (I wrote the story in a separate book called *Seven Years Running*, and am seeking a publisher for that book). However, in this book I want to share with you my background of learning Spanish, watching my mom learn Spanish, and adjusting and growing up in a Latin American culture, because I think many of the lessons we learned in Mexico can be applied in Ecuador, too.

When we first arrived in Mexico, we didn't speak any Spanish, we had little money, and our only contacts there were the family members of Juan, an acquaintance who dropped us off in his little village. Juan stayed around and helped us adjust for the first few weeks, but soon he had to get back to his job in the U.S., so we were on our own.

I remember picking up my first Spanish words as I made friends with the kids in the family we were staying with. I learned *"otra vez"* after giving a little three-year-old a piggy back ride around the house. When I put him down he said, *"¡Otra vez, otra vez!"* I thought, "That must mean 'again'" so I said *"¿Otra vez?"* and he nodded and said *"¡Sí!"* so I picked him back up and took him for another ride!

Being in a new country felt like being thrust into an unfamiliar room in the middle of the night after the light switch had been flipped off! We groped and felt our way around this completely unfamiliar culture, never knowing what we might run into next. I remember being served a big plate of beans and some tortillas our first day there. I was so hungry and so happy for the food, but when I took my first bite of beans I began to cry.

"Ow, the beans are so spicy!" I was so grateful when somebody offered me some fruit, but then they put salt and lemon juice and chili powder on it! Everything was spicy hot! Even the candy that the children ate had chili powder in it.

A day or two later we went to the *mercado*—market place. It took us awhile to get there because we caused a traffic jam—most of the people in the village had never seen Americans before so they all halted mid-step to stare at us! Finally we arrived at the market, which was not your typical Albertson's with its food neatly packaged and arranged in perfect rows on the shelves. In this open-air market, all the produce, beans, rice, meat, and fish lay heaped in piles out in the open!

We walked past one smelly fish stand and I gagged. I turned my nose away, desperately searching for some untainted air to inhale and found myself looking straight into the lifeless eyes of a pig's head, hanging on a hook at a meat stand. Nausea overtook me and I spun around right there in front of the multitude of onlookers and lost my spicy beans all over the ground. I felt completely mortified.

My mom, too, experienced the pain of culture shock. Nobody in this small town owned a washing machine, but having previously lived out in the country near the Canadian border without electricity and running water, she was experienced at washing laundry by hand. After a few days, the time came to wash our clothes.

As she pulled out our laundry and set things up to wash it, a crowd of Mexican ladies began to gather around to watch. Proud and confident of her laundering skills, my mom grabbed a dress and began washing it with enthusiasm.

Instead of the looks of admiration my mom had expected, the ladies gathered in a tight little group, exchanging knowing glances and whispers. *"Ella no sabe* (She doesn't know)," they were saying. My mom couldn't understand them, but she realized that they seemed to think she didn't know how to wash clothes, and by Mexican standards she didn't.

In Mexico, most routine chores have a prescribed "right way" of doing the task. "The Way" is passed from generation to generation. Conformity is prized over individuality.

After a few moments, one of Juan's sisters stepped forward, pushed my mom to one side and snatched the dress from her hands. She sprinkled powdered soap over the garment, and with a motion peculiar to the clothes-washing routine of Mexico, proceeded to wash the garment right side out, frequently pouring small bowls of water over the garment. She then turned the garment inside out and repeated the entire process again, turned the garment right side out again, did a few more rinses. When she had wrung out the water, she gave the dress back to my mom with a gesture that said clearly, "And *that* is how you wash clothes."

My mom, feeling humiliated over a petty difference of technique, misinterpreted the lady's action as hostility and implied superiority. She didn't bother to hide her feelings. When the women stayed around to see how she would do with the next article, she stubbornly sat and did nothing.

The women gestured encouragingly for her to wash, but she refused to do anything until they left. That foolish pride and ignorance cost her their friendship. They interpreted her refusal to recognize the correctness of their way as a statement of her own superiority.

The next day, when my mom began to do the dishes, the same sister who had performed the clothes-washing demonstration angrily pushed her out of the way and washed the dishes herself. My mom's other attempts to help yielded the same result.

Over time, relations with Juan's family were patched, in part due to Juan's efforts and explanations, in part to the natural graciousness of the Latino people, but mostly to my mom's change in attitude. She was learning that the universe did not revolve around Americans, and that wounded pride was not necessarily a bad thing.

As the weeks passed, we started to understand Spanish. My sister and I learned mostly through play, but we watched our mom work a lot harder at it. She took a notebook to the plaza, talked to all the people she could, and wrote pages and pages of notes. Over time she built up a huge vocabulary, even better than many of the locals!

With the understanding of the language came an understanding of the culture. The light in our dark, unfamiliar room flipped back on. Things that might have seemed rude to us as Americans were not necessarily rude in the Mexican culture. Overwhelmingly, people expressed true concern for our well-being and over time we developed close friendships—some of which have lasted to this day. Some people treated us as though we were members of their own family.

At the end of five years, we returned to the U.S. By this time I had thoroughly adopted the Mexican culture, and Spanish had actually become easier for me than English. As an American, I thought I knew my own culture, but five years is a long time when you're only thirteen, and reverse culture shock turned out to be harder than the initial culture shock of moving to Mexico! On the outside I looked and sounded American, but inside I had all these experiences which made me different.

I later learned that there is an actual term for what I was: a Third Culture Kid. TCKs are people who have spent a significant part of their developmental years outside of their passport culture, and consequently have a different worldview than people inside either culture. If you or someone you know is a TCK, access the TCK information and resources in the bonus companion website at **http://www.LilyAnnFouts.com/lojabonus**. This will also be valuable if you plan to move to Ecuador with children, who will soon become TCKs!

We continued to live as fugitives for two more years after our return to the States, but eventually the FBI caught us and my sister and I were forced to return to our abusive father while my mom went to jail. It was the roughest time of my life. In spite of everything, though, I wouldn't trade my life for anyone else's, and I've said it many times: Mexico is the best thing that ever happened to me. To listen to a 30-minute dramatized telling of my story and read a free excerpt from my other book, *Seven Years Running,* visit the companion website. (Gain access via **http://www.LilyAnnFouts.com/lojabonus**.)

In college I majored in Spanish and education, achieving my childhood dream of becoming a teacher. After graduating, I taught for three years in elementary schools, went on to teach Spanish at a community college, and finally found my true joy as an educator teaching classes to adult learners in workplaces where they could immediately apply what I taught. I love helping people with different cultures and languages to connect and build trust with one another.

Since we married in 2011, my husband and I have worked and traveled all over the world. We live in a motorhome, have no permanent home anywhere, and my career has switched to writing and other more portable endeavors.

In 2014, we decided to move to Ecuador for awhile. After doing some research, we decided on Loja. I was a little nervous, having traveled, but not spent more than a month at a time in Latin America for over twenty years.

Would I be able to make friends? Would anyone laugh at my rusting Spanish? Would the people be as kind and wonderful as they had been in Mexico? I can be a shy person in new or unfamiliar social settings, so getting out and mingling with random people does not come naturally to me. How would I get to know people?

The first day after landing in Ecuador I already began to run into some language differences between the Mexican Spanish I had been raised with and the Ecuadorian Spanish being spoken around me now. The food was also different from what I had been raised with in Mexico. Despite these superficial differences, though, I found that the deep Latino culture of generosity, goodwill and family is as vibrant as it was in Mexico. I felt like I had come home.

After a day in Guayaquil, we took the all-day bus ride up to Loja and settled in at the hotel we had reserved for the first night. We planned to spend the next day hunting down a furnished apartment that we would live in for the next two months. I couldn't find anything online, but figured once I was on the ground and started asking around, something would turn up pretty fast.

As it turns out, nobody seemed to know of any places for rent—or even where to look. We walked for miles looking for signs, talking to people, and combing the classifieds in the local papers. We found quite a few unfurnished apartments listed, but nothing furnished for month-to-month rental.

Eventually, something turned up—at a much higher price point than we expected. I'll be sharing more of our house-hunting story and lessons learned in Chapter Eleven on finding a house and setting ourselves up in Loja. I'll just say that things were different on our second trip in 2017, and will continue to evolve on future trips to Loja!

Once we settled into our apartment, we began familiarizing ourselves with the area and trying to find ways to meet people. We hung out in the parks, walked through neighborhoods, and began attending events, fitness classes and yoga classes. We talked to people in the *mercados*. Eventually, people began approaching us and asking us questions. As we became acquainted with them, some invited us to their homes for coffee or a meal.

In the relatively short time that we lived in Loja, we were able to forge new friendships. We loved Loja and its people so much that we returned in 2017 for another six-week visit, got to know our friends better, and made even more friends. We look forward to seeing our friends again on our next trip down!

And now, it is time to introduce you to this lovely city. We'll start with an overview in Chapter Three!

CHAPTER THREE
Getting to Know Loja

　Now it's time to dive in and become acquainted with the beautiful city of Loja. In the following chapters I'll be covering such topics as how to get to Loja, how to get around like the locals, eating and shopping like a local in Loja, things to do in town, finding an apartment and preparing to live there, how to make friends with the locals, cultural differences to expect, the famous nearby town of Vilcabamba, the closest major city of Cuenca, and other surrounding towns and natural wonders within a few hours of Loja.

But first, what is Loja like? Let's begin with a general overview of Loja.

Since we planned to stay in Southern Ecuador for about two and a half months, one of our first tasks upon arrival was to find a place to live. I found a lot of information about Cuenca during my pre-trip research, including listings for furnished apartments for well under $500 per month. I also learned a lot about Vilcabamba, a famous little town–popular with expats–about an hour (by bus) south of Loja. Loja had little information online, but what I did learn about the town intrigued me.

- I learned it was the music capital of Ecuador and had a symphony, which appealed to me because I love live music.
- I learned that Podocarpus National Park was nearby, bio-diverse, and popular with birders, which appealed to me because I love to birdwatch, especially in tropical countries.
- It appealed to both my husband and me because we love mountains and hiking in the great outdoors.
- I learned it had few expats, which appealed to us since we wanted to get to know the locals and their culture.
- I learned that the average daily high temperature was around 70° F (21 Celsius), and never got extreme. This appealed to both of us since I don't like it too cold and Keith doesn't like it too hot.
- I learned that the town had three universities, including one of the top universities in the country, which appealed to both of us because we knew we would be able to find some well-educated people with whom to converse.

City and Province of Loja

The city of Loja is the capital of the large and beautiful Province of Loja—the southernmost province in Ecuador. It is surrounded by Peru to the South, the Zamora-Chinchipe Province to the East, Azuay Province to the North and El Oro Province to the West. It can be confusing at first, because some places may identify as being in Loja—but they may be in a different town in the province. We made this mistake by booking a hotel online in the wrong town when we first arrived in Loja! If you're looking up a business for the city of Loja, look carefully to ensure the place you find is actually in the city and not in fact in a different town in the province!

Climate

Loja's climate is fairly stable throughout the year, usually varying between the 60s and 70s (around 15 to 26 Celsius) for the high temperature and the 40s and 50s (7 to 12 Celsius) for the low temperature. Due to its elevation and position nearly at the equator, the temperature never becomes extreme in either direction. We usually felt comfortable in normal pants and t-shirts during the day.

Loja's place in a valley high in the Andes mountains makes it difficult to predict its weather, even from one hour to the next—especially during the rainy season. It may be beautiful and sunny, but the clouds can roll in quickly and deliver a rainstorm a short while later. Therefore, it is wise to keep an umbrella, poncho, or rain jacket with you when you go out during the rainy season!

The evenings cool off quickly, so carry a light jacket if you plan to be out late. You won't need to pack a thick winter jacket unless you plan to make an excursion up to a higher elevation! Instead, if you plan to be in Loja long-term, pack some clothing that you can layer to adjust for the temperature changes of the seasons. This should include some warm base layers—fleece or wool—for the coldest days and nights of the year, which tend to happen around late June/July. While the temperature never dips below 40°F (4.5 Celsius) even on the coldest nights, the buildings are not heated or insulated and can dip into the 50s (10 to 15 Celsius) inside! Some expats use space heaters for these colder weeks of the year, but the locals tend to just wear warmer clothes and use extra blankets.

The humidity level is an average of 75%—obviously lower during the dry season and higher during the rainy season, when the mornings can be misty. It does not feel overly humid in Loja, especially with its generally cooler temperatures. If you make trips to the Amazon Basin or the coast you will notice a definite increase in humidity compared to Loja!

In 2014, we lived in Loja at the end of the dry season and first part of the rainy season, from late January to the end of March. In 2016-2017, we lived in Loja from mid-December to late January, a season when the weather is mostly nice. For the other months of the year, I have relied on historical records as well as reports from other expats and locals who spend their whole year in Loja.

Safety and Political Climate

During our first stay in Loja in early 2014, we explored all over town and never felt unsafe or threatened anywhere we went. There are certain parts of town where we exercised more caution, such as in the crowded downtown *mercado* and commercial area, as well as around the bus station. We never flashed anything valuable to tempt thieves. Police officers regularly patrol the streets, parks, and downtown area, and seem to do a decent job of keeping everything under control. One even stopped once just to ask us about our experience and make sure that nobody had bothered us.

The second time we stayed in Loja, in late 2016 and early 2017, we also felt very safe most of the time. There was one incident, however, where we felt uncomfortable. We had attended a concert, and at around 9:30 p.m. as we made our way from the theater to the bus stop, we found ourselves next to the downtown *mercado*. The other streets had been brightly lit and full of people, but this street was dark and mostly empty. We noticed a large hooded figure silently staring at us from the shadows about 40 yards/meters away. I interpreted his body language as someone who was sizing us up, and felt threatened. We quickened our pace toward the next street, and I saw a second man ahead of us duck into a gate. As we passed, the man made eye contact with me and urgently motioned to watch out for the hooded figure. I nodded in comprehension, relieved that someone was watching out for us, and we walked briskly to the next well-lit street and joined a crowd of people heading for the bus. The hooded man never followed.

The 'hooded figure' incident illustrates a couple of important points about safety: One, it pays to be aware of your surroundings. Keith and I should have paid attention to where we were walking and stuck to the well-lit streets with more people on them instead of letting ourselves wander onto a dark, empty street. Two, there are good and bad people everywhere. In Latin America, if you are an obvious foreigner, a lot of people are watching you, whether you realize it or not. Many of those people are watching out for your well-being. If a local warns you about a person or place, pay attention.

We aren't usually out late at night, and we did not experience the nightlife in Loja simply because that is not our style. We did go out to the symphony and *Jueves Culturales* (more on that in a later chapter) on many occasions, and with all the other people around and the well-lit streets in the downtown area we felt perfectly safe aside from that one 'hooded figure' incident.

For those who do like to be out and about late at night, exercise the same caution as anywhere else—try not to wander around alone, especially in the more remote parts of town on unlit streets. Drink responsibly, use common sense and remain aware of your surroundings. The locals tell me that the area of town with the most bars and nightlife is quite safe to go out and walk for a few blocks until you can find a taxi home, but as in any city, keep your eyes open.

Only once were we approached by a beggar in Loja in 2014. Unlike many other Latin American countries where I have seen beggars all over the place, in Ecuador—and especially in Loja—they were almost non-existent. Those that do approach do not seem persistent and will usually move on when you say no. On our second trip to Loja, we noticed an uptick in the poverty level. After the devastating earthquake on the coast in 2016, many people, left with nothing, migrated to other parts of the country. Beggars are still relatively uncommon, but several people did approach us asking for money.

Our Ecuadorian friends told us that their government does a good job of taking care of the poor, and that we do not need to feel obligated to give money to beggars. (*Generally, giving money to beggars does not help anybody long-term and only encourages further begging and dependence. Find other ways to help.*)

We never had occasion to call the police, so I can't comment on their efficiency for responding to emergencies, but I have heard that the response time is usually very good. The number to call in Loja is 9-1-1, just like the U.S. The operators will probably not speak English, so if you can't speak Spanish, you'll need to pass the phone to someone who can. (Note that some cities in Ecuador may use a different number. Be sure to check for each city you travel to.)

During both trips, we happened to be in Loja during an election period—in 2014 when the mayor was elected, and in 2017 during the presidential campaigns. Everything ran smoothly both times. Like many other cities throughout the world, groups of people sometimes hold political demonstrations and protests, but these have been peaceful affairs in Loja. There are many who are disgruntled with their elected officials (pretty much like anywhere else in the world), but Ecuador is by and large politically stable at the moment. The Ecuadorians in the mountain region especially pride themselves on their peacefulness.

Overview of the Remainder of this Book

Before anything else, in the next two chapters I will cover some techniques for learning and improving your Spanish. Knowing the local language is a must if you plan to spend a significant period of time in Loja, and even if you only plan to travel through for a few days, knowing a few basics will help a lot. Few people there speak English fluently, and they all appreciate it when you communicate with them in Spanish. Furthermore, understanding the language will help open a door into the culture for you, and give you experiences that you would never have otherwise. Trust me when I say that it is well worth the effort. I have taught many Spanish classes in the past and will share my knowledge and experience to help you jump start your mastery of the language in Chapters Four and Five.

If you don't have your own vehicle, traveling to Loja —and getting around in the town—can be done in several different ways. There are regular buses connecting Loja with the rest of the country, and these are an extremely inexpensive way to travel. Any road in or out of Loja is winding and mountainous and travel by bus can take awhile, but the scenery is amazing. Try to secure a window seat so you can enjoy a nice view and a little fresh air if you're prone to car sickness. Another much faster and more expensive way to reach Loja from Quito or Guayaquil is to fly to Loja's airport, located about 45 minutes outside the city. I'll be talking about transportation to and from Loja in detail in Chapter Six, and I'll also talk about getting around Loja in a taxi and where you might want to stay during your first few days in Loja.

Within Loja, it is easy and cheap to get around on a city bus. The bus system might be a little confusing to someone just arriving in Loja, but there's no need to worry, because I've mapped every route in the entire city bus system for you! In so doing, I not only learned where each bus went, I also learned a lot about Loja's many neighborhoods. I'll cover how to get around on the buses and taxis and describe the different parts of the city in Chapter Seven.

And now for the fun part: what can you do in Loja? Music lovers can rejoice, because Loja is the musical capital of Ecuador. They say in the city that "every home has a musician." I enjoyed many free concerts by the symphony orchestra, weekly Thursday night music and dance performances during *Jueves Culturales*, and for those who like to stay up late, there are other venues in the town that play late night concerts on the weekends. Additionally, Loja has festivals, other art venues and events, cathedrals and museums to explore. In Chapter Eight, I'll discuss these and other activities that you can enjoy in Loja.

If arts and urban adventures aren't enough to satisfy you, Loja is a wonderful place for people who enjoy the great outdoors. There are numerous opportunities for hiking, birdwatching, and outdoor sports and exercise in the many parks inside the city and mountains surrounding it. In Chapter Nine, I'll talk all about the nature that you can enjoy in and around Loja.

Once you're in Loja, you'll want to know where to eat and pick up the things you need to settle in. Like anywhere else in Ecuador, you can easily pick up a local style meal for around $2.00 to $3.00. Loja also has restaurants serving other types of food, usually at a higher price point. Inexpensive food can also be found from street vendors and in the *mercados*, and if you have your own kitchen, the weekly open-air markets are the cheapest place to stock up on groceries. While you're in Loja, you might also want to pick up some gifts or souvenirs for yourself or your loved ones. You might also want to shop for services, such as haircuts, laundry services, or medical services. I'll cover eating, shopping, and services—including medical care—in detail in Chapter Ten.

After arriving in Loja and orienting yourself to the food and fun, you may be ready to start house hunting. This can be an intimidating process. We struggled with this when we first arrived, and we ended up in a less-than-ideal apartment (not for its location or convenience, but for its price). In Chapter Eleven, I'll walk you through different resources you can use to find an apartment or house to move into, should you want to live in Loja for a few months or longer, and hopefully you'll learn from our own experience and have more success than we did on the first try! I'll also share resources for setting up the utilities and internet, getting a phone, finding furniture, and more.

Something else probably on your agenda is making friends. Get out and enjoy the activities you do the most, and interact with the people you meet doing those same activities. By finding people who share things in common with you, you'll open doors for friendships to happen naturally. In Chapter Twelve, I'll share stories of how we made some of our friends in Loja, and ideas to get you started on finding friends of your own.

Once you spend time in the culture and start making friends, you'll begin to uncover some cultural differences. Things that are important in our culture—punctuality, efficiency, individuality—will be different in Ecuador. You'll find that events often start much later than scheduled, and nobody seems to mind. This can be particularly frustrating for North Americans and Europeans when we want to get something done. Any construction projects, paperwork, and other things may not be done to the standard and timeline that you're accustomed to back home. In Chapter Thirteen, I'll outline some cultural differences you can expect to encounter as you settle into life in Loja.

Because of the cultural and language differences, you'll probably experience periods of frustration where you just want to hang out with other expats and speak in your mother tongue for a bit. There's nothing wrong with that! The great thing about Loja is that if you need a cultural break and want to relax in English for a day, Vilcabamba is only a short ride away and is full of expats who can speak English and can probably relate to your frustrations. I caution against getting stuck in the trap of socializing exclusively with other expats and complaining and building walls between yourself and the locals, but spending time with people of your own culture who can understand you can help ease the inevitable stress of living in a different cultural world. In Chapter Fourteen, I'll talk about Vilcabamba—things you can do there, and how it compares to Loja as a place to live.

This book would not be complete without a discussion of Cuenca, since Loja and Cuenca are often compared to each other in blogs and forums around the internet. Pros and cons certainly exist for either city, and expats have overwhelmingly cast their vote for Cuenca as the more desirable place to live. There are already many books written about this beautiful city, so Chapter Fifteen will be a more in-depth comparison, exploring which city may be more appropriate for you depending on your tastes.

Aside from Vilcabamba and Cuenca, many other interesting towns and attractions lie within a half-day journey of Loja, and spending a day—or several days—outside the city can make for a nice change of scenery and climate! Chapter Sixteen will touch on a handful of these towns and things you can do there.

Hopefully this overview of Loja and how to fit in to the local culture will be helpful for you and give you a clear idea of whether or not it would be worth your time and money to get to know Loja personally. Whether you're interested in Loja as a place to travel for vacation, spend a few weeks or months, or even move to permanently, I hope the information in this book will enrich your experience not only in Loja, but in Latin America as a whole.

Let's start off with that important prerequisite: Spanish!

CHAPTER FOUR

First Things First: Learn Spanish!

    Tourists visiting Loja for a few days could find ways to get by with little or no Spanish. For the casual visitor who does not speak Spanish at all, I highly suggest investing a few dollars in a basic travel phrase book and learning a few essential phrases before traveling to Loja. Any amount of Spanish will greatly enhance your experience in the region, since very few people there speak English!
    As I've already mentioned, Spanish is an important prerequisite for *settling* in Loja. If you already speak the language, you're welcome to skip over to Chapter Six!

However, if you don't speak Spanish and you plan to spend significant time in Loja, I would encourage you to begin learning Spanish now. I hope the tips in the next couple of chapters will help break it down into manageable steps for you!

Learning Spanish in Loja
Several people have asked me, "Is Loja a good place to learn Spanish?"

My answer is that it depends. Like any other language learning setting, Loja has its pros and cons.

Loja could be a very challenging place to learn Spanish if you're starting from scratch. The expat population there is still small and very few of the locals speak English, so you'll be thrown into a situation where you will need to use at least some Spanish right away. It might help to have some people around who can help you become oriented to the language and explain things for you as you begin to learn, and you may not have that luxury in Loja.

As you may recall from my chapter on growing up in Latin America, we had Juan to help us during our first couple of weeks in Mexico, but we were thrust pretty quickly into a situation where we were forced to learn the language! Knowing a few basics before being on your own is extremely helpful.

Ron Keffer, reader of the first edition of my book, wrote to me after their exploratory trip to Loja. "Ann and I met exactly two English speakers in Loja," he said, "so, out of necessity, our Spanish improved."

Ann and Ron had been learning some Spanish on their own before traveling to Ecuador, so they weren't starting from scratch. If you spend time mastering some basics before you go, and you interact with people every day while you are in Loja, it can be a great place to learn, for several reasons.

First of all, there is nothing like immersion and just getting out and speaking with people. You'll start out with a lot of sign language but if you force yourself to *speak* with the locals every day, I believe you can break through and pick it up. Ron reported, "The best Spanish teachers we met were the taxistas! They almost always were open to a conversation, and when we told them we were working hard to improve our Spanish, very often they spontaneously would begin a Spanish lesson from which we would take a word or expression or two. There was a good bit of laughter at our gaffes, but we found the taxistas, and just about everyone else in Loja, to be delightful. Even the guards at museums and the like were friendly and helpful when we attempted our very rough Spanish with them."

Secondly, there are some universities in Loja, so you could probably find one or more students studying English who would be happy to trade English lessons for Spanish lessons. "The daughter of the family from which we rented our flat was a 19-year-old English learner, so we arranged lessons during which she helped with our Spanish and we helped with her English," said Ron.

Thirdly, Lojanos speak very good, clear Spanish. If you are looking for a place where the locals generally speak a high quality, well-educated version of the language, Loja is a great choice. They tend to enunciate clearly and express themselves very well. In some regions of Latin America, people speak Spanish with unusual accents, leaving off sounds at the ends of the words and making heavy use of slang, which makes learning the language more challenging. Lojanos have their own peculiar expressions, but their language is excellent. Bottom line: Interaction with the locals is key. You have to be willing to get out of your comfort zone and make a fool of yourself, because that's exactly what someone learning a new language sounds like—a fool. You have to learn to get over it, laugh at yourself, and keep talking with people! If you don't interact with anyone, you will never have more than a book knowledge of the language.

If that sounds too scary for you, you may benefit from moving to a place with more of an expat community where you will have some support, and take some Spanish classes, then think about moving to Loja after you've mastered the basics of the language. Just don't let that expat community be the crutch that keeps you from ever learning Spanish!

My Language Learning Philosophy

If you've read my earlier chapters, you know I learned Spanish as a child and have spent several years of my professional life teaching Spanish in various contexts. Most rewarding to me was teaching Spanish to professionals who found it useful in their line of work—medical and dental professionals needing to speak with patients, supervisors needing to speak with their employees, and school staff wishing to communicate with students and their parents, to name some. These people needed to learn a specific, specialized set of Spanish phrases, and they needed to learn them fast so they could use them in the real world right away.

In teaching these classes, I came to realize that this method of language learning could be useful as a precursor to learning an entire language. The important piece of the puzzle was for them to learn something they could use in the real world—and then go use it right away. Forget the confusing grammar rules to start with and just learn something you can use. The grammar studies can and will come later.

I've put this philosophy into practice several times in my travels to countries where the language was neither Spanish nor English. As an adult learner, I have memorized phrases in Romanian, French and Swahili so that I could interact with locals in their own languages while traveling in their countries. Now I am learning some Thai phrases for our future trip to Asia. I have spoken with many language learners much older than me who do the same, and I have taught many retirees in my Community Spanish classes. Age does not matter!

Learning doesn't have to wait until you reach Latin America. Wherever you are in the world, you can start learning Spanish! In fact, if you arrive in Latin America with some Spanish concepts and phrases already in your mental pocket, you'll be set up to learn even faster.

It bears repeating: Do NOT obsess about the grammar. The best way to learn a language is to actually speak and use it, and start immediately—don't worry about tenses, verb conjugations, masculine and feminine, or plural and singular. Such details will paralyze you and slow you down from reaching the real goal, which is learning to communicate ideas. Learn to understand and be understood, without worrying about saying everything without error. When you learned your first language, you did not study grammar first. You just wanted to communicate your needs and wants! Simply focus on communicating.

You'll mess up, just like a toddler learning to speak

their first language, but the more you actually practice and speak the language, the faster you'll improve! Some language learners actually have a goal to make a certain number of mistakes every day as they learn. Why? Because the more they're speaking, the more mistakes they're making, and the faster they are learning! If you're working with someone who can help you learn Spanish and ask them to point out your mistakes to you, you'll begin making those mistakes less frequently.

In this chapter I'll provide a list of items you should learn, Spanish learning tricks and resources, and some suggestions for what you can do to get started with learning Spanish.

There are certain skills, sets of phrases, and vocabulary words that everyone should know, such as:
- Pronunciation
- Numbers
- Greetings and social niceties like "Please" and "Thank you"
- Comprehension and communication phrases and strategies
- The most commonly used words in the language
- Phrases for common, every-day scenarios such as shopping, ordering a meal and getting around town

There may be specific phrases you'll want to learn for your own personal needs. For example, I am a vegetarian, so whenever I travel to a country whose language I do not speak, one of the phrases I always learn to say is "I am a vegetarian," or "I cannot eat meat." If you have any specific dietary or medical needs, you'll want to be able to communicate those to the people you meet. Everyone is different, so there are certain things you'll want to learn in Spanish sooner than later—and those things may not be the same as what someone else needs to learn.

Order of Attack

Here's a list of steps you should take for self-directed Spanish learning:
1. Learn the basic rules of pronunciation. This can be done fairly quickly since Spanish is very consistent.
2. Learn the main social greetings and niceties that you would use in virtually every encounter on a daily basis.
3. Learn the numbers, since you'll use these daily to communicate prices, time, dates, ages, passport numbers, and much more.
4. Think of the transactions you're most likely to engage in on an extremely regular basis (for example: shopping, eating out, taking a taxi, etc), and memorize the phrases you'll need to know to "get by" in each scenario.
5. Learn some communication strategies for "controlling" a conversation so that you can understand better.
6. Begin learning the 1,000 most frequently used words in Spanish (you'll already know quite a few from the work you've done in Steps 1-5), ideally within the context of phrases and sentences you would use in real life.
7. Learn some common "fill-in-the-blank" sentence patterns that will help you quickly communicate a wide range of information.
8. As you start to notice patterns in the language and wonder why words and phrases are structured a particular way, it is time to begin learning the grammatical rules behind the language.

9. Hopefully by this point you'll be in a position to live in Loja or some other Latin American city for awhile, and you can fully immerse yourself in the language, holding daily conversations and transactions with the locals until you achieve full fluency.

I'll elaborate on each of these steps in the next chapter, but first let me share some principles for language learning that you should apply throughout each step of the process.

(To watch an excellent video on the principles of language learning, visit the companion site. Access it at **www.LilyAnnFouts.com/lojabonus**.)

Principles for Language Learning
1. Speak Daily

First and most importantly, you should be *speaking* the language *daily* throughout the entire learning process, starting out with the first step. Speak the sounds and the words out loud with another person. Find someone who speaks Spanish to coach you through the pronunciation of the words and phrases and converse with you in Spanish.

If you don't know of any willing person, then check sites online such as **meetup.com** and see if there are Spanish clubs in your area. Consider starting one if there are none. There are also various online language learning communities (such as **livemocha.com** and **italki.com**) where you could teach some English in return for someone else teaching you Spanish or pay someone for lessons. With technological advances such as Skype and Google Hangouts, there is no excuse for not speaking a language face-to-face anymore!

If nothing else, pair up with another friend who is also

interested in learning Spanish and help each other. Just make sure you are using the language out loud with someone, because if you're holed up in solitary confinement as you learn, you'll probably experience a major brain freeze when it comes time to actually start interacting with people in the language. Get used to dialogue from the very beginning. After all, the whole point of language is to exchange ideas and information with others.

On days when you can't speak Spanish with another person, at least review your phrases out loud on your own. Talk to your cat! Do whatever it takes, but speak at least a little Spanish every day.

2. Practice Consistently

Secondly, you need to practice regularly and consistently. You don't need to make it a full-time job, but you'll be a more effective language learner if you devote an hour every single day rather than an entire day once a week. As you advance through the steps, keep practicing what you learned previously as you add in new words, phrases and concepts. Write down the words and phrases that you're learning on little flash cards or on a flashcard app on your smartphone and pull them out of your pocket or purse to review whenever you have a minute or two on your hands—waiting in line, stuck in traffic, etc. Drill yourself every day.

3. Engage All the Senses

Third, engage as many senses as you can during your language learning process. Expose yourself to books, music, movies, software programs, and as many conversations as possible. Read it and write it, but most importantly speak it and listen to it. Most of your interaction in Latin America will be with the spoken language, not the written language. Get up and act it out with your body as you say it. Connect motions and physical or mental images to the words and phrases you're learning. If a Spanish word makes you think of an unrelated English word, make a vivid mental image with a story that will help you remember the word and its Spanish meaning. Switch your social media settings to Spanish. Label the items in your house with their Spanish names. Keep yourself surrounded and immersed!

4. Repetition, Repetition, Repetition!

Finally, repetition is key to importing the important phrases you need to know into your long-term memory bank, especially when you're first starting out. Repeat phrases until you are saying them in your dreams at night. Repeat them until you feel like you couldn't possibly repeat them again, and then repeat some more. Vary your practice. Repeat using different voices (sing-song, whisper, growl, normal voice, etc). Repeat in front of a mirror. Repeat with a study partner. Repeat into a voice recorder and then listen to the phrases multiple times, too. Repeat with flash cards throughout the day. Repeat a sentence over and over until it just pops out without you even having to think about it.

For links to recommended apps and websites for learning Spanish, including links to slang terms unique to Loja and Ecuador, visit the companion website. Gain access at **www.LilyAnnFouts.com/lojabonus**.

Now let's start learning Spanish, step-by-step!

CHAPTER FIVE
Nine Steps to Speaking Spanish

Let's get started with a few basic Spanish rules, phrases and strategies right here! Feel free to tackle this in small spurts. Come back to this chapter and spend a little time each day learning more. This is far too much to accomplish in a single sitting, but hopefully you'll find it a useful resource! You can skip any sections you are already comfortable with. Let's do it!

Step 1: Spanish Pronunciation
Let's learn the general pronunciation rules for Spanish.

Spanish is great because once you learn a pronunciation rule, you can trust that there will not be tons of exceptions like there are in English! I'm reminded of my college days when a friend wrote down a word on a piece of paper and showed it to me. The paper said "GHOTI."
"What does that say?" my friend asked.
"Goatee?" I guessed.
"Nope. It says 'fish.'"
"How so?"
"GH as in 'rough,' O as in 'women,' and TI as in 'nation,'" he said smugly.

Rest assured, there will be no such mental gymnastics in Spanish. The toughest part will be to avoid applying your English pronunciation to the Spanish letter. Almost everyone who learns Spanish as an adult will have an accent, but proper pronunciation (accent aside) is achievable by virtually anyone (except maybe someone with a speech impediment). Most Spanish letters are pronounced pretty much the way English letters are, but here are the ones that are different:

The Spanish Vowels
A, E, I, O, and U--are pronounced "ah," "eh," "ee," "oh," and "oo" respectively.
- Always pronounce the A like the A in arch (ah).
- Always pronounce the E like the E in egg (eh).
- Always pronounce the I like the I in tortilla (ee).
- Always pronounce the O like the O in taco or nachos (oh).
- Always pronounce the U like the U in flute or tune (oo).

The important thing to remember is that each vowel only has one sound, unlike some of our English vowels, which can start out with one sound and "glide" into another sound.

The long "A" for example starts out saying "eh" and then glides into "ee," as in the word "acorn." The "U" sometimes starts out sounding like "ee" and then glides into "oo," as in the word "university." (In fact, *universidad* is commonly mispronounced by English speakers who try to apply their English pronunciation rules. It is pronounced "oo-nee-vair-see-DAHD"—*not* "yoo-nee-vair-see-DAHD.")

Spanish vowels are always pronounced the same way–there are no "long" and "short" vowels like we have in English. A is always "ah," E is always "eh," and so on.

The Spanish Consonants

Luckily, most of the consonants are pronounced in a similar way to English consonants. There are just a few exceptions, and here they are:
- The letter G has hard and soft sounds. The hard G is like our English hard G in the word "garden," but the soft G is pronounced like an H, much like in the word "gila monster" (*HEE-lah* monster). Don't give it a "J" sound like we do in English. The G is soft when it is followed be E and I (not by any other vowels). It sounds like "hay," and "he." To make a hard "gay/ghee" sound, you spell it like this: GUE/GUI. This is one instance where the U is silent. The sounds "gway" and "gwee" are pretty rare in Spanish, but you distinguish them with the special u with dots over it: Ü. Using this special U (güe/güi) tells the reader that the U is not silent (example: *pingüino* - penguin).
- The letter H is silent in Spanish, like it is in our

English words "hour" and "honor." You pronounce the word as though the letter were not even there. For example, the word *hora* (hour) is pronounced "ora."
- The letter J sounds like our English H. You've probably heard of *jalapeños*, or maybe *San José*, California, or even *Loja*, Ecuador!
- The double LL. Although the single L is pretty much the same as in English, the double L is pronounced similarly to our English Y. Most of us are familiar with *tortillas* and *quesadillas*. Maybe some of us have even vacationed in *Puerto Vallarta*, Mexico. The LL used to even be treated as a separate letter in the Spanish alphabet with its own section in the dictionary, however that changed many years ago.
- The letter Ñ is the only letter in the Spanish alphabet which does not exist in the English alphabet. It sounds like the "ny" in canyon or the "ni" in onion and union. Maybe you've seen it in *Cañon City*–a town in Colorado, or *La Niña*–one of Christopher Columbus's three ships, or the *El Niño* climatic phenomenon that happens every few years.
- QUE and QUI are used in Spanish to make the sounds "kay" and "key." It's pronounced like in our words "bouquet," and "quiche." The U is silent. Like the U in "gue" and "gui" (see above), many Americans may be tempted to say "kway" or "kwee." If you need to say "kway" or "kwee," spell it CUE and CUI. (The letter K is rarely used in Spanish.)
- The letter R seems to be the most dreaded of the

Spanish consonants. The rolled R, which you often hear when a word begins with R or when there is a double "rr" inside the word, is difficult for many foreigners to pronounce. Although your inability to properly pronounce the R may instantly give you away as a foreigner, you'll still be understood, which is the most important thing to keep in mind. Don't worry too much if you can't get it just right. The R is not always rolled. Sometimes it is "flapped," similar to the way we Americans flap our tongue against the ridge inside our mouth when we say the "tt" in the words "letter," and "butter," or the "dd" in "ladder." Generally you roll the R when it appears at the beginning of a word, and "flap" it when it appears in the middle of a word.

- The letter X usually sounds just like our X in English, but once in awhile they pronounce it like an H. For example, *México* is pronounced "MEH-hee-co." This is uncommon, but something to be aware of. Occasionally there are other ways to pronounce the X, too, but they are so uncommon that we won't worry about those here.
- The letter Z sounds like an S in Latin America. In Spain it is pronounced differently, but we'll focus on Latin American pronunciation here. Perhaps you have heard of *pozole*, a popular soup in Mexico. It is pronounced 'posole' (and often spelled that way in the States). The Spanish word for zone, *zona,* is pronounced "SO-nah."

Accent Marks

Another key to proper Spanish pronunciation is knowing where to put the emphasis when you're saying a

word. In Spanish, emphasizing the wrong syllable of a word could actually change its meaning! There are some general methods for pronouncing Spanish words with and without accent marks–knowing which part of the word to place the emphasis on (in other words, which part of the word to say the loudest). The basic rules are:
1. If a Spanish word ends in a vowel, N, or S, emphasis is placed on the second-to-last syllable in the word, regardless of how long the word is.
2. If a Spanish word ends with any other consonant besides N or S, emphasis is placed on the final syllable, regardless of the length of the word.
3. Accent marks override the first two rules. Emphasis should always be placed on the syllable that has the accent mark. Also, if the emphasis is placed anywhere but the last or second-to-last syllable in any word, that word should have an accent mark in it.

Placing the emphasis on the proper part of the word is important, because sometimes emphasizing a different part of the word can change the meaning entirely. Not to be gross or anything, but for example, in Spanish, the word for vomit is vómito. However, if you spell it vomito it means "I vomit," and if you spell it vomitó it means "you/he/she vomited." Another common word that changes meaning with an accent mark is el papa/el papá (the pope or the dad). There are also some single syllable words whose meaning changes depending on whether or not they have accent marks, for example "si" means if, while "sí" means yes; and "el" means the, while "él" means he or him—though that's more of a change in writing than in pronunciation.

Accent Mark Rules

Table 4.1

Rule 1 (vowel/N/S)	Rule 2 (other consonants)	Rule 3 (accent marks)
vo**mi**to (I vomit)	vomi**tar** (to vomit)	v**ó**mito (vomit)
tra**ba**jan (they work)	traba**jad** (work [command])	traba**jó** (he/she worked)
limpio (clean)	limp**iar** (to clean)	lim**pió** (he/she cleaned)
grapas (staples)	ve**loz** (fast)	l**á**piz (pencil)
persistente**men**te (persistently)	telefon**ear** (to phone)	tel**é**fono (telephone)

That's it for the major differences between Spanish and English pronunciation! See if you can find a Spanish speaker to pronounce each of these letters and accented words for you and give you some more example words for each one. For some additional resources—including links and videos for learning pronunciation—visit the companion website to this book. (Access at **www.LilyAnnFouts.com/lojabonus**.)

Step 2: Greetings and Niceties

Now that you've got the basic pronunciation rules mastered, learn a few phrases you can use when you meet people and conduct transactions. You may already know these common Spanish greetings and social niceties! It's important to learn these to break the ice and establish initial trust with the people we talk to.

A quick note on my phonetic pronunciation guide: pronounce each syllable just as it looks. Syllables are separated with dashes (-). In some cases you will see a plus symbol (+). In those cases it is joining two sounds within the same syllable, so you should say the two sounds quickly. For example, the word for silence—*silencio*—would be phonetically spelled out as see-LEN-see+oh. It is a three-syllable word, and the final syllable is pronounced something like "syoh," rather than as two syllables. Syllables that should be emphasized are written in capital letters.

Here are the most important greetings to learn:

Common Greetings
Table 4.2

English	Spanish	Pronunciation
Hello	Hola	OH-lah
Goodbye	Adiós	ah-DYOSE
Good morning	Buenos días	bway-noce DEE-ahs
Good afternoon	Buenas tardes	bway-nahs TAR-dess
Good evening/night	Buenas noches	bway-nahs NO-chase
See you later	Hasta luego	ah-stah LWAY-go
See you tomorrow	Hasta mañana	ah-stah mah-NYAH-nah
Have a good one!	Que le vaya bien	kay lay VAH-yah bee+EN
How are you?	¿Cómo está?	CO-mo ess-TAH?
Fine, thank you	Bien, gracias	bee+EN, GRAW-see+ahs
And you?	¿Y usted?	ee oo-STEAD?
What's your name?	¿Cómo se llama?	CO-mo say YAW-mah?

English	Spanish	Pronunciation
My name is...	Me llamo...	may YAW-moe...
Nice to meet you	Mucho gusto	MOO-cho GOOSE-toe
Likewise	Igualmente	ee-gwall-MEN-tay

Politeness is important all over the world, and the Spanish-speaking world is no exception. If you come across as rude and distant, you won't win the trust or admiration of the people in Loja or anywhere else in Latin America. A little "please," "thank you," "excuse me," and "I'm sorry" can go a long way. Here are some social niceties worth learning right away:

Social Niceties
Table 4.3

English	Spanish	Pronunciation
Please	Por favor	pour fa-VORE
Thank you	Gracias	GRAW-see+ahs
Thank you very much	Muchas gracias	MOO-chahs GRAW-see+ahs
You're welcome	De nada	day NAH-dah
It's not a problem	No es problema	no ess pro-BLEH-mah
Just a moment	Un momento	oon mo-MEN-toe
Excuse me (coming through)	Con permiso	cone pair-ME-so
Pardon me (interrupting, etc)	Perdón	pair-DOAN

I'm sorry	Lo siento	Lo see+EN-toe
Delicious	Delicioso	day-lee-see+OH-so

Practice these interactions with a friend or Spanish tutor! Make flashcards and drill yourself until you can say them all by memory, without hesitation.

For more resources visit the book's companion website. (Access at **www.lilyannfouts.com/lojabonus**.)

Step 3: Numbers

There's hardly an aspect of life where numbers don't come up. You'll need to use them for telling time and dates, conducting financial transactions, learning ages, giving passport numbers, addresses, and so much more. Here are the numbers, followed by four ideas for practicing them.

Numerals and Spanish Pronunciation
Table 4.4

Numeral	Spanish	Pronunciation
1	uno	OO-no
2	dos	dose
3	tres	trace
4	cuatro	QUA-trow
5	cinco	SINK-oh
6	seis	sase
7	siete	see+EH-tay
8	ocho	OH-cho
9	nueve	NWAY-vay
10	diez	dee+ESS
11	once	OWN-say
12	doce	DOE-say

13	trece	TRAY-say
14	catorce	caw-TORE-say
15	quince	KEEN-say
16	dieciséis	dee+ess-ee-SASE
17	diecisiete	dee+ess-ee-see+EH-tay
18	dieciocho	dee+ess-ee-OH-cho
19	diecinueve	dee+ess-ee-NWAY-vay
20	veinte	VEIN-tay
21	veintiuno	vein-tee-OO-no
22	veintidós	vein-tee-DOSE
23	veintitrés	vein-tee-TRACE
24	veinticuatro	vein-tee-QUA-trow
25	veinticinco	vein-tee-SINK-oh
26	veintiséis	vein-tee-SASE
27	veintisiete	vein-tee-see+EH-tay
28	veintiocho	vein-tee-OH-cho
29	veintinueve	vein-tee-NWAY-vay
30	treinta	TRAIN-tah
31	treinta y uno	train-tah ee OO-no
32	treinta y dos	train-tah ee DOSE
40	cuarenta	qua-REN-tah
50	cincuenta	seen-KWENN-tah
60	sesenta	say-SEN-tah
70	setenta	say-TEN-tah
80	ochenta	oh-CHEN-tah
90	noventa	no-VEN-tah
100	cien	see+EN
101	ciento uno	see+en-toe OO-no
200	doscientos	dose-see+EN-tose
300	trescientos	trace-see+EN-tose
400	cuatrocientos	qua-trow-see+EN-tose

500	quinientos	key-nee+EN-tose
600	seiscientos	sase-see+EN-tose
700	setecientos	say-tay-see+EN-tose
800	ochocientos	oh-cho-see+EN-tose
900	novecientos	no-vay-see+EN-tose
1000	mil	meel
1,000,000	un millón	oon mee-YOAN
2,000,000	dos millones	dose mee-YO-nace
3,000,000	tres millones	trace mee-YO-nace
0	cero	SAY-row

Here are four ideas for practicing the numbers:
1. For numbers one through ten, take a deck of playing cards and use them as flash cards. Remove the face cards. If you have a language learning partner, play against them. Whoever calls out the correct number first keeps the card; most cards wins.
2. For numbers two through twelve, practice by rolling dice and calling out the number as quickly as possible. To play against a partner, have a stack of pennies, poker chips, beans, or some other small token. Whoever calls the number correctly first receives a token. Most tokens wins.
3. For the multiples of ten (10, 20, 30, 40, etc.), use the playing cards and pretend each number has a zero after it. (So 2 becomes 20; 6 becomes 60; etc.) Do the same for multiples of 100 (so 2 becomes 200; 6 becomes 600; etc).
4. For random two-digit numbers (e.g. 53, 19, 42, 67, etc) put two playing cards together (take out the 10s

to avoid confusion). So if you randomly draw an 8 and an ace, it would represent the number 81: *ochenta y uno*. If you drew an ace and a 5, it would represent the number 15: *quince*. Do this for three-digit numbers, too, if you like!

Keep on practicing and drilling yourself until you can say the numbers in Spanish without hesitation! For more resources visit the book's companion website. (Access at **www.LilyAnnFouts.com/lojabonus**.)

Step 4: Most Useful Phrases
As you're planning out your Spanish learning strategy, be conscious about the phrases you will use regularly and what your greatest needs will be. One of the key concepts to *quickly* learning enough Spanish to get by in the real world is that less is more. Don't overwhelm your brain with 370 phrases. Choose wisely the phrases that you know you'll use practically every day and memorize those. I recommend an absolute maximum of 50 to start with.

Sit down and think through the typical scenarios you'll be most likely to encounter. What phrases will you say most often? For example, you'll probably be conducting some kind of shopping transaction on most days. Phrases that you're likely to use in that scenario might include, "How much does it cost?" and "I want that one, please."

Spend some time thinking about which scenarios you expect to find yourself in most often. In Loja, some likely daily situations would be shopping, eating out, taking a taxi or bus, and asking directions. Write down any likely situations you can think of, then write down all the important phrases you can think of for each scenario on a separate index card for each phrase. Try to distinguish between "nice-to-know" phrases and "*need*-to-know" phrases.

Next, take your stack of high-use phrases and prioritize them. There are several ways in which you might choose to do this, depending on your needs.

One way is to prioritize in order of most used to least used. Think of the Pareto Principle. Which 20% of the phrases in your list will you use 80% of the time? Order your sentences accordingly, and then begin learning your most used phrases first.

A second way to prioritize might be to first put your sentences into logical groups. Group your sentences according to each situation. Once you have all your phrases grouped by situation, prioritize the groups in order with the most common situation at the top.

A third option for prioritizing is to look not at the most used sentences, but the most critical ones. Maybe you use some sentences more, but other sentences are actually more important to you—for example, maybe you have a severe allergy that you need to be able to tell people about.

Eventually, of course, you'd like to learn all your phrases, but by prioritizing you increase your effectiveness from day one. Arranging your phrases into a logical order also helps to break the learning task into manageable steps that you can start tackling right away. Choose the method that makes the most sense for you and get started!

But where can you find your Spanish phrases? One of the best sources for commonly used phrases that are helpful to any newcomer to a country are phrase books, such as the Berlitz travel phrase books. Pick one up and find specific phrases you know you will need to say over and over again and learn those first.

If there are phrases you feel are necessary but you can't

find them in a phrase book, write them down and find a Spanish translator to translate them for you. If you can't find one around town, post a question to the forums at **WordReference.com** or pay someone $5 to translate your phrases on **Fiverr.com**. If you've never used Fiverr before, use my referral link **(http://bit.ly/lilyfiverr)** for a free $5 gig. (Access this link and all other links in this chapter in the companion site at **www.LilyAnnFouts.com/lojabonus**.)

Just remember to focus your efforts where the payoff will be greatest, actually practice these with a real person, and study for a little while every day.

Step 5: Communication Strategies

Be a control freak. The more of a beginner you are, the more important this strategy is. In order for you to be able to carry on two-way communication with any degree of success, you not only need to be able to make yourself understood, you also need to be able to understand what the Spanish-speaker is trying to say to you. I have a hearing loss and I have to ask "what?" a lot. With Spanish, you may find yourself doing the same thing. Having them repeat, slow down, or explain themselves in a different way may help you to understand much better. Here are a few "control" phrases to learn:

Speak more slowly, please.
Hable más despacio, por favor.
AH-blay MOSS dess-SPA-see+oh pore fa-VORE.

Repeat, please.
Repita, por favor.
ray-PEE-tah, pore fa-VORE.

I don't speak much Spanish.
No hablo mucho español.
No AH-blow MOO-cho ess-pah-NYOAL.

I don't understand.
No entiendo.
No en-tee+EN-doe.

Show me, please.
Muéstreme, por favor.
MWAYS-tray-may, pore fa-VORE.

This last phrase is useful if the Spanish speaker is trying to explain where something is or trying to describe anything that they can easily show you. You can have them point out a place on a map, physically take you somewhere, draw something with a pen and paper, or pull out a physical object to show you.

If you need to obtain some information from the Spanish-speaker, avoid open-ended questions at the beginning. Do not ask things like, "What happened to you?" or "What did you do yesterday?" Once they begin to answer, you'll wish you'd never asked. Instead, learn to ask questions that have a yes or no answer. "Did you have fun yesterday?" "Is this your little girl?" Then when they answer, you'll get it. If it is important that you understand what they are trying to tell you and they begin to rattle off an incomprehensible story, politely ask them to answer with yes or no:

Answer with yes or no, please.
Responda con sí o no, por favor.

Ray-SPONE-dah cone SEE oh NO, pore fah-VORE.

Of course, yes/no questions aren't always possible, so if you must ask an open-ended question it should be one in which their answer can be short and limited, such as a number ("What time is it?" "How much does this cost?"), a day or date ("What day will the concert be?"), or another question that would give a simple, definite answer ("Where are you from?" "What is your name?"). Don't let them tell long stories unless you want some Spanish listening practice and it's not critical that you understand everything. Bring the conversation back under control.

Another strategy is the age-old charades game. When they can't yet speak a language, most people rely on physical gestures and facial expressions to get their message across. It might look silly, but it's effective! There's a lot you can do with just a little bit of Spanish if you can tap into your inner mime and act things out.

Step 6: Top 1,000 Words

Your next task is to begin memorizing the most commonly used words in Spanish. Above I referenced the Pareto Principle, which states that in many cases, 20% of our actions account for 80% of the results we receive. This is true of language, too! Did you know that just 20% of words make up roughly 80% of all day-to-day language? Words like "the," "and," "in," "because," etc, are used much more frequently than words like "theoretically" and "kiwi."

If you can learn just the top 1,000 most frequently used words in Spanish, you will be a *very* significant way along the path toward being able to speak and make sense of the language. Make some flash cards or use Anki (**https://apps.ankiweb.net**) and start drilling yourself. Try to learn these words in context as much as possible. If you are working with a Spanish tutor ask them to give you some example phrases with these words in them—especially phrases that you would likely use in day-to-day life.

The good news: you'll notice many words that are very similar to English, and thus very easy to learn!

For a link to the Top 1,000 Spanish Words—including their pronunciation—visit the book's companion website. (Access at **www.LilyAnnFouts.com/lojabonus**.)

Step 7: "Fill-in-the-Blank" Formulas

This step can be done nicely in conjunction with Step 6. As you continue learning various phrases, you'll start to notice word and sentence patterns and recognize words so you can put them together in new sentences. You can jump-start this process by intentionally seeking out formulas in the sentence structure. Here are some examples:

"*Esto*" means "this." You can combine the word "this" with action words to express a lot of commands, without having to learn the name of each object you're referring to. Simply learn the command, and then say "*esto.*" For example: Put this on, Read this, Drink this, Eat this, Move this, Clean this, Fix this, I need this, I want this, Throw this away, etc. If you're referring to more than one item, say "estos" (these). The basic formula, with examples below, is:

[Action Command] + [this/these] + ["stuff" (optional)]
Lea (read) + *esto* (this) + *por favor* (please).
Lleve (take) + *estos* (these) + *a la casa* (to the house).

The "stuff" can be anything like an expression of time (e.g., "Do this *now*"), a person or place (e.g., "Take this to *Señor Torres*"), or any other words that would help to complete the sentence so you can communicate what you need to say. "Stuff" is optional in many cases. Write down the super relevant commands you might need to use and make your own cheat using this formula!

A similar concept to using "esto" phrases is to find other sentences that you can use over and over and just change one or two words in a fill-in-the-blank style. The following formula uses what I call the D.I.N.A. words because they express Desire (want to), Intent (going to), Need (need to/have to), or Ability (can). By learning the DINA words and the basic formula, you can simply plug in relevant words—it's much faster than trying to learn the proper conjugation of every single Spanish verb. (If you don't know what I mean by that, don't worry about it. Just learn these formulas!)

Here's the master formula with some examples below:

[DINA word] + [action] + ["stuff"] + [./?]
Necesito (I need) + *limpiar* (to clean) + *esto* (this).
¿Puede (Can you) + *reparar* (repair) + *esto mañana* (this tomorrow)?
Queremos (We want) + *ir* (to go) + *al parque* (to the park).
¿Van a (Are y'all going) + *comer* (to eat) + *la sandía* (the watermelon)?

Just like the "esto" phrases, the action is any action a person could do, and "stuff" is usually optional and it's just any words that help to complete the sentence. In these

DINA phrases, the "stuff" might actually be the word "esto"! The sentence can be changed to a question simply by changing the tone of your voice from a command or statement to a question tone, with a rising inflection at the end. Fortunately, these are yes/no questions, which make it easy to understand the reply!

To download my complete list of DINA words and a comprehensive list of "esto" phrases, visit the companion website. (Access at **www.LilyAnnFouts.com/lojabonus**.)

Step 8: Grammar Time

Once you recognize patterns in the language, you'll wonder why a sentence is worded one way rather than another. At this point it is helpful to begin studying the grammar to make sense of the language and understand the underlying rules. Now you can visit the academic textbooks and learn the gritty details behind all those confusing things like gender and number agreement and verb conjugation. Many language textbooks start out with these grammar rules, but I have found that with most of my students they only hinder learning until they use the language enough to put the grammar rules into some kind of context. Put the language into action, *then* learn the rules behind it. For a list of recommended grammar books and resources, visit the companion website. (Access at **www.LilyAnnFouts.com/lojabonus**.)

Step 9: Full Immersion

At some point during this process you will travel or move to Loja or somewhere in Latin America (or so I assume, since you're reading this book). At this point, whether it is early on in your step-by-step process or many months after you have begun learning Spanish, you will be able to fully immerse yourself in the language and hold daily conversations with native speakers.

Once you've mastered the basics of a language (Steps 1-5 in particular), immersion becomes a useful aspect of the language learning process. You'll also pick up on slang terms and regional expressions that may not exist in any Spanish language textbooks. Visit the companion website (access at **www.LilyAnnFouts.com/lojabonus**) for links to some slang and expressions you'll encounter in Ecuador and in the Loja region. The more you spend time with the locals, the more comfortable and fluent you will become in Spanish! I'll be covering some strategies and offering resources for getting to know the locals in Loja in Chapter Twelve.

If you're serious about learning Spanish or *any* new language, I highly recommend the book *Fluent in 3 Months* by Benny Lewis. It is full of great ideas for learning a new language, and contains special sections on specific languages, including one on Spanish. It is the best language learning book I have ever read. Don't let the audacious title scare you off. Go to this URL to order it on Amazon: **http://amzn.to/1KpHBpg**

Now that you have a game plan for learning the language, it's time to visit Loja. Even if you're not yet fluent in Spanish, the locals will appreciate your attempts to learn. Many people in Loja do want to learn English and will be happy to work with you and meet you halfway. With a few Spanish basics under your belt, you're ready to explore! In the next chapter we'll talk about arriving and getting around in Loja.

CHAPTER SIX

Arriving in Loja and Finding Your Way Around

One of the things I love about Latin America is how easy it is to travel around without a car, and Loja is no exception. With frequent bus service to and from the town, regular city buses, numerous taxis and a decent pair of legs to get you to the main roads in town, you can easily go from one end of the city to another in well under an hour, or quickly step onto a bus out of town to any part of the country. In this chapter we'll cover the ways you can travel to Loja, set up your temporary base, and find your way around town in a taxi.

Getting to Loja

If you're flying into Ecuador, you'll probably land in Quito, in the northern part of the country or Guayaquil, near the coast. To travel from either of these cities to Loja, in the Andes mountains in the southern part of Ecuador, you can either fly or take the bus. Flying will cost much more, but will also save you a tiring road trip. Flying may also be a better option if you're prone to sickness on the curvy mountain roads. If the weather is nice, the flight over the Andes is gorgeous, but you'll miss the amazing up-close scenery of the road!

Buses
Personally, I enjoy buses. I like to watch the countryside go by, and occasionally I'll have a fun conversation with a fellow passenger. It gives an up-close view of the country, and it's the way many locals travel—but it's all a matter of personal preference. I know some people hate buses.

If you've traveled in other parts of Latin America, you may know that the quality of buses can vary tremendously. Mexico has a range, including some luxurious buses that I would ride before a Greyhound bus any day, while Nicaragua and Guatemala have retired school buses crammed with families of five in seats originally intended for two children.

Ecuador's buses tend to be middle of the road. They are proper buses meant for longer trips—not school buses. Some are newer and cleaner than others, and they are generally in good repair, but not always.

During our 2016-'17 trip to Loja, our bus to Zamora broke down on the way out of town. Where in the United States many disgruntled passengers would be yelling about missing appointments and wanting a refund, the

Ecuadorians just sat back and took it in stride while the driver grabbed a wrench and went to work under the bus.

A few minutes later, the driver came back and started the bus, but the motor choked to a halt as soon as we began moving forward. He grabbed his tools and returned to the underside and we heard more metal clanging.

Another bus from the same company passed us on its way to Zamora as we sat there. Nobody yelled at the driver for not asking the other bus to stop and take on the passengers. After two more tries, the driver succeeded and we continued on our way to Zamora, driving around the curves at breakneck speed to make up for lost time. Eventually we caught up to the bus that had passed us and both buses made it to Zamora at about the same time.

I also had the misfortune of a broken seat back on my first ride in Ecuador, from Guayaquil to Loja, back in 2014. The seat would not come to the upright position and was permanently reclined. Fortunately the bus was not full, so I simply moved to another seat. Ecuadorian buses are not usually overcrowded except during special events when lots of people are traveling at once. Most Ecuadorians travel by bus, so service is frequent.

The buses are generally comfortable. They may or may not be equipped with A/C, though this doesn't matter so much if you're traveling in the mountains and the windows can be opened for cool air. Some buses are equipped with restrooms, but they usually keep them locked and when you ask to use them they try to make you wait for their next stop. One time, after drinking way too much water, I couldn't take it any longer and insisted that they let me in.

"Urine ONLY," they instructed. I nodded.

The bus assistant unlocked the door for me and waited

outside while I did my business (awkward, but normal for Latin America). Peeing on a moving bus is challenging while the bus careens around the winding Andes mountain roads, but thankfully the handlebars made it doable. The bathroom on that bus was in decent condition. Buses generally make restroom stops at regular enough intervals that most people won't feel the need to use the one on the bus if there is one. Most of the public restrooms that we stopped at while riding the buses were quite clean and well-maintained.

If you decide to take the bus, you will need to get from the airport to the bus station in Quito or Guayaquil. You'll probably want to book a night in a hotel, since most flights arrive late at night, and get to the bus station the next day.

The bus station in Quito (known as *Quitumbe*) is about an hour away from the airport and there is a city bus that goes from one to the other. The cost is $1.50. A taxi will cost quite a bit due to the distance. You can buy a ticket all the way to Loja (a 12 to 14-hour trip) or break it up by riding to Cuenca, staying overnight, sightseeing a bit, and going the rest of the way the next day. The cost is around $20 for a bus ticket from Quito to Loja.

In Guayaquil the bus station is right by the airport, so it is much easier. It is a nine-hour trip and bus tickets cost around $12.

Unlike the social side of Ecuador, which pretty much ignores the clocks, buses almost always depart from the station on schedule.

A handy website to see the bus schedules from all over the country can be found at **http://andestransit.com**.

Loja's main bus station (*Terminal Terrestre*) is located on the north side of town. When you arrive, you'll see a host of taxis waiting for you out front, as well as a city bus stop near the pedestrian bridge.

Flights

If you decide to fly from Quito or Guayaquil, you'll land at the Loja airport (LOH), which isn't actually located in Loja, but in Catamayo about 45 minutes away.

That is, you will *probably* land at the Loja airport. If the weather is bad, as it was when my mother-in-law and sister-in-law came to visit us, your flight may be diverted. It can get very rainy in the mountains, and when we woke up the morning our family members were scheduled to arrive, sheets of rain pounded the streets and the whole region was socked in with clouds and fog.

I appreciated the safety measure of diverting the flight, but unfortunately TAME's customer service left us all disappointed. We expected that the airline would fly them from Guayaquil to Loja on the next available flight at no additional charge, since Loja was the destination they had paid for. Instead, TAME, the only airline that flies to Loja, refused to give our family members the flight. The best they could do was to offer a flight in two days at $100 per person. It seemed unfair to all of us, but there was nothing we could do about it, so our family ended up riding a bus the next day.

Assuming your flight makes it to Loja, that's the easiest option. Prices range from less than $50 to over $100 per flight, depending on when you buy the ticket, for what dates, and whether you buy one-way or round-trip.

We flew from Loja back to Quito at the end of our last stay in Loja, and everything went smoothly. Our cost was about $50 each. It is a gorgeous flight. Enjoy the view of the snow-capped peaks near Quito!

To get from the airport into Loja, you can take a

private taxi for about $20, or share a taxi with other passengers to split the cost. A budget option is to take a taxi a short distance to the bus station in Catamayo for around $1.00, and then ride the bus from Catamayo to Loja for $1.30.

Leaving Loja

Leaving Loja is simple. There are buses to many destinations around the country—some of the more popular ones depart every few minutes to couple of hours. There are many different bus companies in the *Terminal Terrestre*—the cities they service and departure times are posted where you can see them. Buy your ticket at the appropriate counter and then go through the turnstile gate (which you have to pay a dime to go through) out to the buses which are parked in numbered slots. They will tell you which slot number to find your bus. Remember to check **http://andestransit.com** for bus schedules if you need to plan ahead. Additional resources are on the bonus companion website. (Access at **http://www.LilyAnnFouts.com/lojabonus**.)

To go back to the airport, either take the bus to Catamayo from the *Terminal Terrestre* (it departs every few minutes), then take a taxi from the Catamayo bus station to the airport; call a taxi company to arrange a shared taxi; or hire a private taxi to take you.

Finding a Temporary Base in Loja

I do recommend having your first night in Loja booked somewhere so you won't have to worry about arranging that on arrival, especially if it's late. If you haven't made prior arrangements, ask your taxi driver for a recommendation based on your budget (most *hostales* in town have clean double rooms with private bathrooms for around $20-$25 per night [less for singles], or you can get a more upscale place for more).

A word of caution, as I mentioned earlier in this book: if you're booking online look carefully to make sure you are actually booking at a property in the *city* of Loja, rather than another town within the *Province* of Loja. When we first arrived we discovered we had booked a place in another town over an hour away. We had to cancel at the last minute (no refund) and book one that was in Loja.

We used **booking.com** to secure a room at Hotel Podocarpus (address and phone: *Jose Antonio Eguiguren 16-50 y 18 de Noviembre,* +593 7-258-4912), which is a good multi-story hotel with an elevator right in the downtown area with Wifi, comfortable beds and a good breakfast. At $45 per night, we paid more than double what we would have at one of the "hostales" in town. However, Hotel Podocarpus was a nicer place by comparison and we could rest easy knowing that we had a place to go to when we arrived. There are nicer hotels in town, too, for those who like more comforts.

This year, in contrast to 2014 when we went, there are also an increasing number of options on **Airbnb.com**. For a stay of just a few days, you might consider staying in a private room, which will give you the experience of staying with a local family. If you like more privacy, whole apartments are available, too. Several of them are reasonably priced and managed online for the local owners by an American expat named James W.

If you have not set up an account with Airbnb already, use this referral link to obtain a credit toward your first stay, currently $40: **http://bit.ly/lilyairbnb**

If you plan to live in Loja for a few months, a furnished apartment through Airbnb may be all you need and would spare you from any further house hunting. However, if you plan to move to Loja permanently or spend a significant portion of your year there annually, you may want to find an unfurnished apartment, which will save a lot of money over time after the initial outlay to get it set up. The Airbnb apartments make a great base to work from while you hunt for longer-term options. (For more information on finding a long-term house or apartment, see Chapter Eleven.)

Unless you need a very large place, I recommend not paying more than $30 to $40 per night for a fully furnished apartment. Look for a discount if you're paying by the week, and pay absolutely no more than $550 per month for a three-bedroom or smaller apartment, including utilities. (Unfurnished places should be significantly cheaper than this, especially outside of downtown.)

Finding Your Way Around Town Via Taxi

If it's your first time in Loja, it is easiest to hail a taxi to your accommodations until you can get your bearings with the city bus system.

Taxis in Loja are cheap—$1.25 to $2.00 between the center and anywhere in the main part of town, or $2.00 to $4.00 to go all the way across town or to a neighborhood on the outskirts. Taxis in Loja have meters in them, so make sure the taxi driver turns on the meter before he starts driving. (Exception: Nighttime costs may be a little higher, so if it is late the driver may not turn on the meter.) The minimum charge is $1.25. It's easy to spot the taxis—they are yellow. To stop a taxi, just hold your arm out and wave it to signal you want a ride.

To hail a taxi away from a main route, you can use a smartphone app called *Ktaxi*. It works a little like Uber or Lyft by allowing you to call a taxi to your location from the app (sometimes you need to enter the address to confirm), and showing you where the taxi driver is and their estimated arrival time. The difference is that unlike Uber and Lyft, you cannot pay through the app. You still need to pay the driver in cash.

If you can't speak enough Spanish to give your taxi driver directions to your stop, it is helpful if you have your destination address written down, ideally including a cross-street or landmark in case the driver isn't familiar with the place where you want to go. See if you can find someone to help you with this ahead of time—for example, your host family if you're staying at an Airbnb.

As cheap as they are, if you have a modest budget you may not want to rely exclusively on taxis for your transportation around Loja. The city buses run on a frequent basis to every major region of the city. At $0.30 per ride, you'll save many dollars over time, especially if you're traveling all the way across town, where taxis are likely to charge $2.00 or more.

In the next chapter, I'll tell you all about the Loja bus system and how to use it.

CHAPTER SEVEN
City Buses and Neighborhoods of Loja

Learning how to get around on the city bus system could save you some money and open another perspective on local life. If you plan to spend more than a few days in Loja, and especially if you're exploring the city in search of a great neighborhood to call home, you'll definitely want to become an expert bus rider!

One of the things I enjoy doing most when traveling is to explore a city via its public transportation system, especially if public transport is the primary method most locals use to get around as it is in Loja. I love to jump on a random bus line and ride it to the endpoint, then hop off and explore the area on foot. This practice has resulted in us finding charming neighborhoods, lovely trails beyond the city to hike on, good conversations with the locals, and even new friends.

During our latest trip to Loja, I visited the transportation office begging for a complete map of the city's bus system. They referred me to the tourism office, who referred me back to the transportation office, and so it went. I received a partial diagram of the bus system, but nothing more. There is an Android app called SITU Loja, but since I have an iPhone I wasn't able to test that, either. If you have an Android phone, this app may be worth downloading!

I decided to make my own map. Keith and I spent about 20 hours riding every bus in Loja from end to end in both directions while I ran a GPS tracker and took photos and notes.

What follows is a detailed description of Loja's entire bus system. I hope you find it useful.

The Basics: How to Ride the Bus

Loja's city buses cost $0.30 USD per ride as of early 2017.

Bus drivers and their assistants like people to get on and off the bus as quickly as possible so they can make good time. Get on the bus, hold on to something so you don't fall when the bus takes off (sometimes very abruptly), and find a seat or suitable place to stand. An assistant on the bus will come around and collect the money from the passengers at regular intervals. If you do not have exact change, the assistant will make change for you.

There are some stops in the downtown area where

passengers pay at a turnstile before boarding the bus. The cashier will hand you a small slip of paper with a bar code on it which you scan to go through the turnstile. If you are transferring from one bus to another at one of these stops, you do not have to pay for the second ride if you stay inside the bus loading area.

Outside of the downtown area, buses have designated stops every two blocks along their routes. Look for a blue and white sign that says "PARADA" and has a bus on it. Sometimes buses will stop outside the designated areas if you wave them down, but it depends on the driver.

Some of the less popular routes will not have an assistant to collect your bus fare. If this is the case while you are riding, simply pay the bus driver before you get off. Exact change is appreciated so the driver can focus on driving instead of making change, but they will make change if you need it.

If you ride a bus all the way to the end of a line and stay on board, you are expected to pay the 30-cent fare again for the return trip. At the other end of the line, you'll see a whole line of buses awaiting their turn to leave again. You can observe the bus drivers tinkering around under the buses (doing maintenance work), cleaning their buses, and taking breaks. At these turnaround points, you will be kicked off the bus and can jump on another one leaving at the regularly scheduled interval.

City buses are usually marked on the front windows with the names of the beginning and endpoints of their routes and the neighborhoods and notable sites they pass, as well as a line number, marked as "L-1," "L-2," etc.

All city buses pass through some part of the downtown area, and every route also takes you past the *Terminal Terrestre* (bus station for buses leaving the city).

For my complete city bus system map, visit **http://bit.ly/lojabus**. You can check and un-check the various routes to show them or hide them and zoom in and out to get a more detailed view of the streets and neighborhoods and their location relative to the rest of the city.

Loja's Bus Routes

Loja has nine city bus lines: L-1, L-2, L-4, L-5, L-7, L-8, L-10, L-11, and L-12. (There is no L-3, L-6, or L-9 as of this writing.) Here are the nine routes superimposed on a map of Loja. As you can see, the buses will take you within a few blocks of almost anywhere in the city.

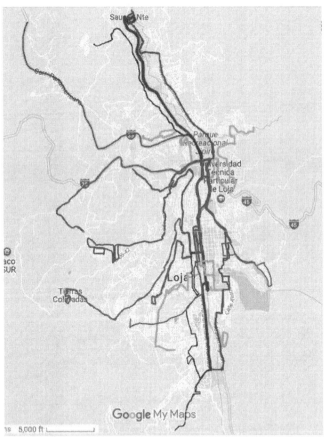

For additional maps, resources, photos, and information related to each route, visit the bonus companion website. (Access at **http://www.LilyAnnFouts.com/lojabonus**.) In the following route descriptions, major points of interest are in bold.

Route L-1: El Rosal - Pitas

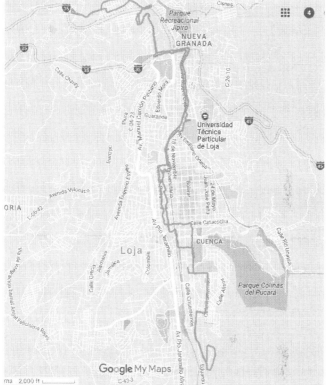

This route begins at El Rosal, a neighborhood in the southeastern part of Loja, and ends in Pitas in the northwestern part of Loja. The neighborhoods and points of interest along this route include:
- El Rosal
- Yaguarcuna
- La Pradera
- Colegio Bernardo Valdivieso
- Cabo Minacho
- Perpetuo Socorro

- Lauro Guerrero
- **Parque Bolívar**
- **Puerta de la Ciudad**
- **Gran AKI**
- **El Valle**
- Calazans
- **Terminal Terrestre**
- Turunuma (ECU 911)
- Mercado del Pequeño Productor
- Las Pitas
- Consacola
- Los Laureles

Buses run every eight minutes from 6:15 a.m. to 6:52 p.m.

El Rosal is a good looking neighborhood with some nice middle class homes and a view of the southern end of Loja.

Las Pitas is a poorer end of town. It has some beautiful views, but a local person later told us to never buy property on the northwest end of town, no matter how cheap, because the ground in that area is very unstable due to a geologic fault line there. Buildings sink into the ground and landslides are common.

Route L-2: Argelia - Sauces Norte

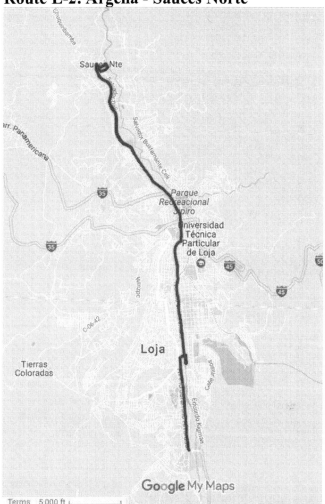

This is the primary route running along Loja's main north-south roads, from the Universidad Nacional de Loja to Sauces Norte. You will likely ride this route most often. The simple north-south route passes the following neighborhoods and points of interest:
- Argelia
- **Universidad Nacional de Loja**
- **Supermaxi/Mall Don Daniel**

- Coliseo
- Los Paltas
- **Plaza de la Independencia**
- Miguel Riofrío
- **Parque Central**
- **Benjamín Carrión (Parque Bolívar)**
- Hospital Isidro Ayora
- Puente Bolívar
- **Mayorista**
- Loja Federal
- **El Valle**
- **Terminal Terrestre**
- Subestación Salvador Bustamante Celi
- **Parque Jipiro**
- Subestación Pablo Palacio
- Los Chilalos
- La Cascarilla
- **Parque Orillas del Zamora/Zoológico**
- Sauces Norte

Buses run every 3 minutes from 6 a.m. to 10 p.m.

The south end of town along this route, between Supermaxi and the university, has some nice middle class neighborhoods where an expat or two have chosen to live. The location next to this regular bus line is convenient, and there are nice walking opportunities along the river and nice views of the surrounding mountains in places where you can look beyond the buildings.

The north end has a poorer and more rural feel, but for the avid hikers there is a beautiful walk to the top of Cerro Zañe which starts from Sauces Norte. Those who enjoy country living might consider this area, on the east side of the river.

Route L-4: Borja - Isidro Ayora

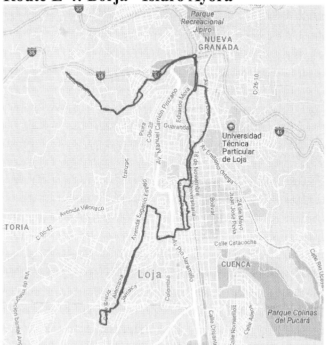

This route sticks to the west side of town, beginning due west of the Terminal Terrestre (bus station) at Borja, traveling east to the bus station, then dropping south into the downtown area before winding up the hill to the west and south and ending up in Barrio Isidro Ayora. The neighborhoods and points of interest along this route include:
- Borja
- Clodoveo
- **Terminal Terrestre**
- Zona Militar
- Ciudadela del Maestro
- **Mayorista**
- **Parque Bolívar**
- Ramón Pinto

- Mercadillo
- Las Peñas
- Miraflores
- Avenida de los Paltas
- Iglesia Divino Niño
- Barrio Isidro Ayora

Buses run every 7 minutes from 6:12 a.m. to 7:43 p.m.

The northwestern part of town is, in general, the poorer part of the city. Despite this, the views as you climb up the hills through the neighborhoods, are breathtaking. Aside from the views, this route does not have any major points of interest that I am aware of.

Route L-5: Colinas Lojanas - Zamora Huayco

This is an east-west route that runs from Barrio Colinas Lojanas high on the western side of Loja, down through Barrio Daniel Alvarez to the roundabout on Pio Jaramillo (near Supermaxi), through the downtown area, then on to

the nice neighborhoods of Rodríguez Witt and Zamora Huayco on the Zamora river on the east side of town. The neighborhoods and points of interest along this route include:
- **Colinas Lojanas**
- ANT
- Daniel Alvarez
- **Mercado La Tebaida**
- Perpetuo Socorro
- Lauro Guerrero
- Parque Bolívar
- Avenida Cuxibamba
- **Mayorista**
- **El Valle**
- **Gran AKI**
- **Terminal Terrestre**
- Ciudadela del Maestro
- Mayorista (again)
- Colegio Beatriz Cueva de Ayora
- **Estadio**
- Carcel
- **Rodríguez Witt**
- **Zamora Huayco**

Buses run every 7 minutes from 6:05 a.m. to 7:30 p.m.

Zamora Huayco is a lovely neighborhood up the Zamora river. If you get off the bus at the bottom of the Zamora Huayco loop/turnaround point, you can follow the road back until it turns into a trail and follow the river for awhile. It's a beautiful walk.

Rodríguez Witt is a wealthier part of town with the biggest and fanciest homes. I heard someone once refer to it as "The Hollywood of Loja."

Mercado La Tebaida, next to the roundabout on Pío Jaramillo and Av. Manuel Benjamín Carrión, is just a few blocks from the Supermaxi, Don Daniel Mall, and the beautiful Parque Lineal Sur "La Tebaida," which is a lovely place to stroll along the river.

As the bus climbs up the hill to Daniel Alvarez, look around at the beautiful mountain scenery. When it reaches the end point at Colinas Lojanas, you can take a short walk to the top of the hill to get a 360-degree view, including the wind turbines and all the mountains surrounding Loja.

Route L-7: Punzara - Motupe

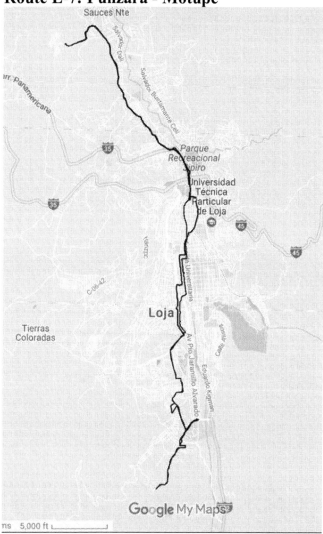

Route L-7 is a north-south route along the western side of town which roughly parallels the more popular L-2 route, except that it ventures farther south into Barrio Punzara. The route begins at Punzara in the south and runs north up to Motupe. The neighborhoods and points of interest along this route include:

- **Punzara**
- Sindicato de Choferes
- Julio Ordoñez
- **Universidad Nacional de Loja (UNL)**
- Ciudad Alegria
- Esteban Godoy
- Heroes del Cenepa
- Centro de Matriculación Vehicular
- Santa Teresita
- Escuela Lauro Damerval Ayora
- Por la Policía
- San Pedro
- Lauro Guerrero
- **Parque Bolívar**
- **Mayorista**
- **Terminal Terrestre**
- Pitas
- La Banda
- Pucacocha
- Motupe
- Barrio La Concepción

Buses run every 6 minutes from 6 a.m. to 8:07 p.m.

Barrio Punzara has a country feel to it although it is still within the city of Loja. The people there seem very friendly. It's a great jumping off point for several nice hikes.

The Motupe end of the bus line is also beautiful, and you'll find places to walk just up the hill from the bus turnaround point. We noticed several alarmingly lopsided homes and buildings in the neighborhood, which is in the area we have been warned about for unstable ground.

Route L-8: Ciudad Victoria - Carigán

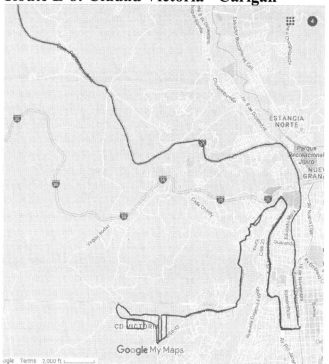

Much like the L-4 route, the L-8 sticks to the west side of town and seems to go through some of the poorer neighborhoods. The neighborhoods and points of interest along this route include:
- Ciudad Victoria
- Clodoveo
- **Plaza de la Independencia**
- **Parque Central**
- **Benjamín Carrión (Parque Bolívar)**
- Hospital Isidro Ayora
- **Terminal Terrestre**
- **Jipiro**
- Iglesia Cristo Rey
- Carigán

Buses run every 7 minutes from 6 a.m. to 8 p.m.

Route L-8 shares some downtown stations with the L-2 and L-11 buses, so if you ride to the "Plaza de la Independencia" station (downtown, where the pedestrian bridge crosses the street) and don't go out through the turnstiles, you can transfer to one of the other buses without having to pay for bus fare a second time. To ride a bus in the opposite direction, cross over on the pedestrian bridge. This will keep you inside the bus station.

Ciudad Victoria is one of the few parts of Loja that felt "rough" to me. It has a great view of the wind turbines, but feels "ghetto-ish" and urban. We never felt threatened or any kind of danger as we wandered the neighborhood, but the graffiti and broken windows on some of the buildings gave me a sense that this area may see a higher rate of crime than other parts of the city. Although I have no statistics to back this up, I would be more careful in this area.

Carigán, like Motupe and Las Pitas, is in the part of town where the buildings tend to shift in the unstable ground. Landslide Central. Although it's a beautiful area and we enjoyed a hike and rapel adventure there with some of our friends, it's not a place where I would buy property or rent long-term.

Route L-10: Sauces Norte - Argelia

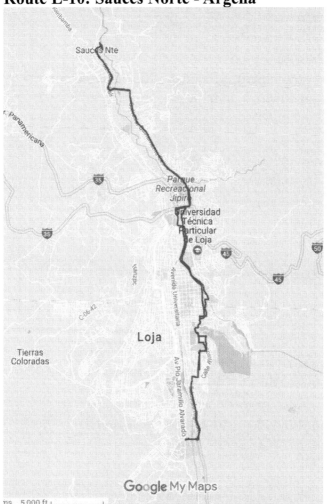

Just as Route L-7 parallels the L-2 to the west, Route L-10 parallels route L-2 to the east, and has the same beginning and end points of Sauces Norte and Argelia. The neighborhoods and points of interest along this route include:
- Sauces Norte
- COMIL

- Colegio Eugenio Espejo
- La Paz
- La Inmaculada
- **Parque Jipiro**
- **Teatro Nacional Benjamín Carrión**
- **Conservatorio de Música S.B. Celi**
- **Terminal Terrestre**
- **El Valle**
- Ciudadela del Maestro
- **Mayorista**
- **Gran AKI**
- Colegio Beatriz Cueva de Ayora
- **Estadio**
- Lourdes
- Colegio Pio Jaramillo Alvarado
- Cabo Minacho
- Colegio Bernardo Valdivieso
- La Pradera
- Yahuarcuna
- **Universidad Nacional de Loja (UNL)**

Buses run every 5 minutes from about 6 a.m. to 8 p.m.

Route L-11: Tierras Coloradas - Bolonia

Route L-11 joins the L-4 and the L-8 on the west side of town. This route also shares some downtown stations with the L-2 and L-8 buses, so from the "Plaza de la Independencia" station you can transfer to one of the other buses without having to pay for bus fare a second time. The neighborhoods and points of interest along this route include:
- Tierras Coloradas
- Chontacruz
- **Plaza de la Independencia**
- **Parque Central**
- **Benjamín Carrión (Parque Bolívar)**
- Hospital Isidro Ayora
- **Terminal Terrestre**
- Belén
- Plateado
- Bolonia

Buses run every 7 minutes from 6:00 a.m. to 7:40 p.m.

It's a pretty ride up to Tierras Coloradas, which is the closest bus route to the wind turbines on the west side of town. However, the turbines are still a good walk beyond them, so it's easier to take a taxi from town unless you're prepared to hike.

A local friend warned us to be careful in the Bolonia neighborhood, which she said has a higher crime rate. I noticed that this neighborhood is next door to Ciudad Victoria which gave me the same feeling. Bolonia is definitely a poorer neighborhood, but beautiful. I enjoyed the quiet and the views of the city and surrounding mountains and was sad to hear that crime has been a problem there.

Route L-12: Sol de los Andes - El Paraíso

This is an interesting route. It starts in the scenic southwestern part of town and ends in a canyon next to the Jipiro River on the northeastern end of town. The neighborhoods and points of interest along this route include:
- Sol de los Andes
- Juan José Castillo
- SOMEC
- ANT

- Época
- Policía
- San Pedro
- Coliseo Ciudad de Loja
- Perpetuo Socorro
- Lauro Guerrero
- **Parque Bolívar**
- **Mayorista**
- **Terminal Terrestre**
- **El Valle**
- San Cayetano
- Samana
- El Paraíso
- Jipiro Alto (La Libertad)

Buses run every 7 minutes from 6:15 a.m. to 7:30 p.m.

I haven't explored either end of this route in depth, but it looks like there could be some promising hiking spots beyond both ends. The southern end has been recommended to us for hiking. Unfortunately, the day we rode this bus, it was raining quite heavily.

Visit the bonus companion site to see more bus-related information and photos, plus city maps and other useful resources! (Access at **http://www.LilyAnnFouts.com/lojabonus**.)

Congratulations! You've made it to Loja and you can get yourself around. Now you're ready to set out and have some fun! That's what we'll cover in the next chapter.

CHAPTER EIGHT

The Fun Side of Loja for Art and Culture Lovers

Loja is mostly unknown outside the country, but it's up-and-coming as a tourist destination. The current mayor (as of 2017) is working hard to make the city even more beautiful and attractive for tourism. It's a great destination for lovers of music and the arts, hikers, birdwatchers, and adventurous travelers who enjoy venturing off the beaten path.

The city of Loja is known within Ecuador as the

cultural capital of the country. Although the larger cities like Quito, Guayaquil and Cuenca may actually have more cultural events, it's impressive what Loja does have given its modest size of less than 200,000 people. I've been astounded at the level of talent in such a small city. Many of Ecuador's most renowned musicians and other artists studied in or came from Loja.

In this chapter, I'll share the activities that you can enjoy related to arts, culture, and the actual city of Loja.

Music

Loja is known nationwide for its culture and music. A famous Ecuadorian song says, "If you haven't been to Loja, you don't know my country." There's a saying around Loja that there's a musician in every home. If you're only visiting Loja for a short time, be sure to enjoy some music before you leave.

Orquesta Sinfónica de Loja

Musicians come from all over the world to perform as guests with the *Orquestra Sinfónica de Loja*, or OSL (Symphonic Orchestra of Loja). Director Andrea Vela of Quito, with a long list of musical accomplishments from multiple countries spanning the globe, skilfully conducts the symphony. Most weeks, the symphony offers a concert free to the public. It is usually at the historic *Teatro Bolívar* (on *Rocafuerte*) or at the brand new national theater, *Teatro Nacional Benjamín Carrión*, just to the east of *Parque Jipiro* (on *Salvador Bustamante Celi*). To see their upcoming events, visit their website at **www.sinfonicadeloja.gob.ec** or the OSL Facebook page at **www.facebook.com/sinfonicaLoja**.

Jueves Culturales

Jueves Culturales is another free weekly event that takes place in Plaza San Sebastián on Thursday evenings from 8 to 10 p.m. This impressive production features talented musicians and dancers of all kinds, with local, national, and international performers. The city broadcasts the show via radio and television. We rarely missed a week. Go see it!

More Live Music

Musicians of all kinds come to play live music in many bars around town, usually late on a Friday or Saturday night. A few venues recommended by expats and local friends include:

- *Zarza Brewing Co.* -
  http://www.zarzabrewing.com
  Address: Calles Esmeraldas y Pto. Bolivar, El Valle
  Phone: 7-2571413
  Email: info@zarzabrewing.com
- *La Huerta* -
  https://www.facebook.com/lahuertagaleria
  Address: Mercadillo 10-78 entre Juan Jose Peña y 24 de Mayo
  Phone: 99 297 8773
- *Lemon Trip* -
  https://www.facebook.com/lemontriploja
  Address: Bernardo Valdivieso entre Imbabura y Quito
  Phone: 98 476 3441
- *La Mancha De Don Quijote* -
  https://www.facebook.com/lamanchadedonquijote
  Address: Bolivar 10-41 entre Miguel Riofrio y Azuay
  Phone: 99 896 6036

Festivals

This being Latin America, there are also regular festivals and holidays to celebrate throughout the year—many of them religious. Here are some of the festivals you may enjoy while in Loja:

Carnaval Weekend: February or March

Carnaval weekend, in February or March (connected to Easter, so the date can vary), is a major celebration, but more so in Vilcabamba than in Loja. Many people from Loja head south to celebrate. If you don't like to get wet, don't leave your house during Carnaval. Water and foam fights are a big part of this celebration, so be prepared. You won't even be safe inside the bus! Kids line the streets, spraying and throwing water onto passing vehicles. If you're sitting next to a window, close it or the people standing by the road may toss a bucket of water into your seat. I wear hearing aids, so I wore a hat that covered my ears during the entire Carnaval weekend to keep them from getting wet. My advice is to prepare yourself and then go out and have fun. We armed ourselves with cans of spray foam so we could fight back! (Read about our experience with Carnaval weekend on the companion site. Access at **www.LilyAnnFouts.com/lojabonus**.)

Pilgrimage of the Virgin of El Cisne: August 17 to 20

The largest festival takes place from August 17 to 20 and attracts hundreds of thousands of people from around the country and even from other countries. At this time of year, Loja is overrun with tourists/pilgrims. If you plan to arrive in Loja during this time it would be wise to secure your accommodations before arriving, and expect the cost to be higher than normal. During this festival there is a pilgrimage from El Cisne—a small village in the province—to Loja, where they carry the *Virgen del Cisne* in stages from one cathedral to the other. The Virgin stays in the cathedral in Loja until November, at which point there is another big festival to carry her back to El Cisne.

Feria de Loja: September 1 to 15

The next festival happens from September 1 to 15 and is the *Feria de Loja*—which seems to be the equivalent of a state fair. There are lots of vendors selling all kinds of products, foods that are unique to the fairs, amusement rides, games, and more. This is the oldest fair in Ecuador.
http://feriadeloja.com

Festival Internacional de Artes Vivas: November

In 2016, Loja held the first annual *Festival Internacional de Artes Vivas* (International Festival of Live Arts), which attracted over 30,000 spectators and performers from around the world. Visitors enjoyed music, theatrical performances, street art, puppetry, crafts, and much more. Everyone I talked to said it was beautiful and made me feel jealous that I wasn't there. The city plans to hold this festival every year.
http://festivaldeloja.com

Independence of Loja: November 18th

The third big festival in Loja is the celebration of Loja's independence, which is November 18th. The night before there is a big celebration in the *Parque Central* with what they call *la noche de luces*, or the night of lights. There are fireworks shows and other festivities that night, and the celebration of independence the following day.

New Year Celebrations: December 31/January 1

In Loja, the New Year celebrations are a much bigger deal than Christmas. In the days leading up to the holidays, we saw lots of vendors selling masks, wigs, costumes, fireworks, traditional candies, and other things in addition to Christmas decorations and gifts. The town was abuzz with chatter about New Year dances and parties.

On December 31, I looked out the window of our apartment and could see our neighbors making preparations for the evening. Everyone was either making or displaying (from their windows or fences, etc) their *monigotes*, also known as *Años Viejos* (Old Years), which are dolls—often life-sized—made of paper or sawdust, dressed in old clothes, and with realistic faces sometimes designed to look like an actual person—sometimes a famous figure or an individual that the creator of the *Año Viejo* knows personally. Some people also strapped their *Años Viejos* to their cars and paraded them around town. These figures represent the old year and will all be burned at midnight.

Keith and I strolled around town to see what people were doing, and saw an alarming number of men dressed as women. These are known as *viudas* (widows), and the tradition is that they are "married" to the *Años Viejos*, but since the Old Years are now dead, the *viudas* go around and beg for money for the funeral costs, etc. The "widows" dress in skimpy dresses and stop traffic, dancing for the motorists and asking for money. It all makes for lots of fun and laughter!

In the evening on New Year's Eve, we enjoyed a concert and dance at *Puerta de la Ciudad* (Gate of the City)—one of Loja's iconic landmarks. Vendors sold hot drinks and packages of twelve grapes from stands around the dance area. The twelve grapes, which everyone eats at midnight, are supposed to bring good luck for the coming year.

When midnight came, the sky erupted in fireworks over the *Puerta de la Ciudad*, and all around the city people lit fireworks and burned their *Años Viejos*, sometimes with notes of negative memories from the last year attached to them. This tradition represents letting go of the negative things from the last year and starting fresh with the new year.

In addition to the big city-wide festivals, each *barrio* (neighborhood) also has its patron saint with related festivities (an example of such a festivity was described to us by Mélida in *Punzara Grande*—see the hiking section in the next chapter). Twenty-six separate celebrations happen in different neighborhoods throughout the city at different times of the year. There are countless other days of celebration, too. Ecuadorians love to celebrate!

More Art and Events

Loja has multiple theaters and exhibit halls where they have different performances, films, and artistic exhibits every month, including paintings, sculptures, and more. Usually, you'll have free admission!

To find out what else is happening in Loja, and when, check the following resources:

- Pick up an *Agenda Cultural* from the tourism office at the Parque Central (on the northeast corner of Bolívar and Eguiguren)
- Visit the *Que Hay en Loja* Facebook page at **www.facebook.com/quehayenlojainfo** to see what's happening. Many upcoming events around the city are mentioned on that page.
- Visit the *Casa de la Cultura Ecuatoriana Núcleo de Loja* (CCE-Loja) Facebook page at **www.facebook.com/cce.nucleodeloja** to see upcoming film screenings, art-related workshops, exhibits, and more at one of Loja's main cultural centers. CCE-Loja is located at the corner of Colón 13-12 and Bernardo Valdivieso. Phone: 7-257-1672.
- Visit the Facebook page, Coordinación Zonal de Cultura, at www.facebook.com/Zonaldecultura7 to check for any other upcoming events.

Museums

Loja also has several museums to explore. For the most part, the signage in the museums is in Spanish. Here's a list:

Puerta de la Ciudad

The most interesting one to look at on the outside is the *Puerta de la Ciudad,* or Gate of the City, located on *Avenida Universitaria.* It has a medieval castle sort of look to it. It was actually only built in 1998, but it's a famous landmark in Loja and has an exhibit inside, a gift/craft shop, a cafe, and a lookout on top where you can climb stairs all the way up and look out over the city. The building was replicated from a coat of arms sent by King Felipe II to Loja in 1571. The city was considered the gateway to the Amazon.

Museo de la Cultura Lojana

Located in the Parque Central is the *Museo de la Cultura Lojana*, or Museum of the Culture of Loja. (It's on 10 de Agosto between Bolivar and Valdivieso. Phone: 7-256-3351) It contains the archaeological, historical and colonial history of the province and the city of Loja. There are seven rooms in the museum, each showing a different aspect of the area including its nature, archeology, important historical figures, art, and more.

Museo de Madres Conceptas

A few steps away from the *Museo de la Cultura Lojana*, you'll find *Museo de Madres Conceptas* at 10 de Agosto and Calle Bernardo Valdivieso. This is in a 17th century convent from the colonial era. The museum contains pictures, household utensils, and tools used by the nuns for self-flagellation. It also houses a collection of works of religious art.

Museo de Arqueología y Lojanidad

This archaeological museum on the campus of the *Universidad Técnica Particular de Loja* houses some 1,600 artifacts, many from the pre-Columbian period. There are three floors in the museum, with artifacts organized according to their age. On the first floor are Paleolithic and Neolithic artifacts and remains of the Valdivia culture. The second floor contains artifacts from the Tolita, Jamás Coaque, Bahía, and Guajala cultures. The third floor exhibits items from the Carchi, Imbabura,

Panzaleo, Puruhuá, Casholoma, Tacalshapa, Manteña, Tardía, Milagro, Quevedo, Huancavilca, and Inca peoples.

Museo de Música
Located downtown on *Bernardo Valdivieso* between *Rocafuerte* and *Riofrío*, this museum houses exhibits on the musical history of composers and performers from Loja, from Renaissance to the avante-garde. The collection spans almost 200 years of history, with more than 7,000 musical scores and 65 instruments on display.

Museo Matilde Hidalgo de Procel
The museum, located on Imbabura and Lauro Guerrero, near Isidro Ayora Hospital, houses artifacts from the life of Matilde Hidalgo, the first woman to become a medical doctor in Ecuador, and also the first woman to vote in Latin America.

Museo de Arte Religioso San Juan del Valle
This museum of religious art is located on the corner of Salvador Bustamante Celi and Guayaquil in the Iglesia de El Valle (the church). Four different rooms display paintings and works of metal and wood. The paintings, sculptures, and other works of art date back to the 18th, 19th and 20th centuries.

Churches
The primary churches in Loja include:

La Catedral
Built in 1838 in a colonial style, this church is one of the largest in Ecuador. It's in the *Parque Central* on the

corner of Valdivieso and Eguiguren. The original cathedral was built of adobe in the 1500s but was lost to earthquakes. The cathedral houses the *Virgen del Cisne* every year for the famous pilgrimage, from August 20 to November 1.

Iglesia de San Francisco

This small church on the corner of Bolívar and Colón was built in 1548 and rebuilt in 1851. In front, it has a monument to Alonso de Mercadillo, the founder of the city.

Iglesia de Santo Domingo

This church was originally built in a Gothic style in 1557, but an 1867 earthquake destroyed all but the twin towers. The church was then reconstructed in a colonial style, with the original spires remained as a reminder of the earlier construction. See it on the corner of Bolívar and Rocafuerte.

Iglesia de San Sebastián

This church, located in the *Plaza de San Sebastián*, also known as the *Plaza de la Independencia*, was built in the year 1900. The city of Loja had been consecrated to Saint Sebastian in 1660 in order to prevent destruction by earthquakes. The church shares its plaza with the tall clock tower which commemorates the November 18, 1820 declaration of independence from Spain.

Explore the City

- A double-decker tour bus leaves from Plaza San Sebastian three times per day and costs $7 per person. The information is all in Spanish, but it's a

fun (if somewhat harrowing, thanks to the low-hanging cables you must watch out for if you're on the top deck) way to see the historic center of Loja. The ride lasts 90 minutes, goes through the historic center, and climbs up to a lookout point for a good view of the city. There are usually very few tourists on the bus, and most of them are from other parts of Ecuador or South America.
- From the Plaza Central, Plaza San Sebastian and Parque Jipiro (and more locations to come!) you can rent electric bicycles for $0.90 per hour or $5.50 per day! If you enjoy exploring on two wheels, grab a bike and ride the streets and parks of Loja.
- One of my favorite ways to explore a new city is to ride around on the public transportation. Hop on a city bus (see Chapter Seven) to a turnaround point and explore on foot to see what treasures you find. Enjoy amazing views of Loja and the surrounding mountains as you ride up the hillsides!

I'll talk more about the hikes at the end of some of the bus routes in Chapter Nine. Get ready to delve into the natural activities Loja has to offer!

CHAPTER NINE
The Fun Side of Loja for Nature Lovers

In addition to the beautiful music and wonderful cultural opportunities Loja has to offer, I believe the region's greatest asset is its natural beauty. For people who love nature, birds, and long hikes in the mountains, Loja is paradise. In this chapter, we'll cover the natural side of Loja, starting with the parks in the city and moving on to bigger hiking adventures beyond the city limits.

Parks

I love parks! Green spaces bring a bit of nature into the concrete jungle of the city, encourage people to enjoy the outdoors and exercise more, and provide a lovely place for friends and family to socialize in wholesome ways. As a traveler, parks are among the first things I seek out in a new city. They are usually free, and they provide opportunities for me to watch the locals during their happy moments of relaxation–parents playing with their children, friends playing a sport, or young couples in love sitting by a pond and feeding the fish and ducks.

In Ecuador (and throughout Latin America), weekends and holidays are busy times in the parks. Especially when the weather is nice, friends and families flock to the recreational areas of their cities and enjoy the opportunity to visit, celebrate, and play together.

Loja, Ecuador is lucky to have several nice parks within its city limits. Here are the ones worth noting:

Parque Jipiro

The largest city park in Loja is one of the most famous and recommended attractions in town. It contains many replicas of buildings from around the world. The buildings have various functions, from administrative offices to game rooms for kids to an old train converted to an internet cafe. We enjoyed the big slide on the building designed to look like a European castle. The kids found it amusing that adults like us went down the slide.

There is a pond with an island housing various types of birds–flamingos, geese, a peacock–and you can rent a paddle boat. We had a great time paddle-boating around the pond and man-made lazy river in 2014. The cost is $3.80 for a half hour. The boats fit up to 3 adults, or one adult and three children, or two adults and two small children.

Jipiro also has a large indoor swimming pool and an outdoor gym for people who want to work out.

During the weekends, you can also enjoy a short ride on horseback through the park. It costs $1.50 for a 10-

to 15-minute ride, or $1.00 for pony rides for small children eight years old or younger.

As I mentioned in the last chapter, electric bicycles are also available for rent beginning at $0.90 per hour, which could make a fun way to explore the park's trails.

North of the park, trails follow the river for four kilometers to another park we enjoyed: *Orillas del Zamora* (a.k.a. *La Banda*—more information below) and continue from there up to the *Sauces Norte* neighborhood. It's a beautiful walk, and relatively flat if you like to walk but find the steep mountain trails too intimidating. We have heard some reports of foreigners being mugged along this trail, so I recommend using caution by walking the trail during the weekends when there are many other people around, finding other people to walk with so that you are not by yourself, and of course staying away from the area after dark. We have walked the trail numerous times ourselves without a problem.

Orillas del Zamora/La Banda

This park contains the city zoo (in 2014 it was a 75-cent entrance fee; it's now $2 for adults and $1 for kids), an orchid garden, a go-kart track, a playground, picnic areas, etc. The trail from Jipiro follows the river through this park and continues northward.

The go-kart track, called the "kartódromo," is open every day from 10 a.m. to 6 p.m. and $5 will give you 7 laps around the track, or 4 laps if you have a child with you. On Wednesdays and Thursdays they have a two-for-one special.

The zoo has been a special topic of controversy recently. The wonderful mayor, Dr. José Bolívar Castillo Vivanco (he goes by *"El Chato"*), has made many improvements in the city since we were there three years earlier. The trails in several parks have been cleaned up and extended, he has improved the city bus system, and he is putting the utilities underground to eliminate the hazardous and unsightly overhead power lines and cables running through the city. He is there for the people, and gets out and mingles with the citizens and takes a personal interest in the projects he is working on for the city. We saw him often at the weekly *Jueves Culturales* performances. By and large, the citizens seem happy with the mayor's changes, though there is a fair amount of grumbling over the increased taxes and fees they have to shell out to pay for it.

One of El Chato's "pet" projects (pun intended) is to improve the city zoo. One of the ways he has done that, according to the disgruntled friend of ours who was telling us about it, is by raising $200,000 in a campaign called *Jirafatón* (Giraffathon) to buy and transport two giraffes to the Loja zoo.

We saw signs and billboards for this campaign all over town. There were even two giant neon giraffes on top of the *Puerta de la Ciudad* at the city-sponsored New Year's party.

"We had a giraffe once before and it didn't survive," our friend said. "This is not the proper climate for giraffes. The enclosures at the zoo are small, too. It makes me sad to see the animals in captivity there."

I talked to several other friends about *Jirafatón* and every single one of them seemed displeased about it.

"That's a lot of money that would be much better spent on something else," was the general sentiment.

The zoo is a fun place to spend a couple hours and watch the monkeys and ocelots play, but it's small and, in my opinion, not really worth a special visit for a shorter trip to Loja.

Parque Lineal del Sur "La Tebaida"

This is the first park we encountered after our arrival in Loja, and special to us since we lived right next to it for two months. It's on the south side of town, near Supermaxi. Following the Malacatos river for a couple of kilometers with trails on either side, much like the trails at *Parque Jipiro*, this park also has several scenic bridges across the river and a climbing wall. Like *Jipiro*, *La Tebaida* also has an outdoor gym for people who want to work out and lots of playground equipment for the kids. We also heard that they were bringing more electric bicycles to the city and that this park would be a place where you could rent them, so watch for them when you go!

Between our first visit in 2014 and our visit in 2017, the trails along the river have been extended for many kilometers on both sides. One can now hike up one side of the river to several kilometers north of the *Universidad Nacional de Loja*, cross the river on a small bridge and walk all the way back on the other side of the river. In my opinion, it's an even more beautiful walk than the trails north of *Jipiro*, and also relatively flat compared to most other hiking spots in the area.

Parque La Tebaida is popular with families during evenings and weekends. There are always lots of people exercising on the trails or in the gym area every morning. On Sundays people bring in large inflatable jungle gyms for the kids to play on and the vendors come through selling snacks and drinks. Guys gather to play volleyball games. It's a fun place to people-watch. Sit down to watch a volleyball game and you may end up having conversations with the other spectators.

Parque Colinar Pucará Podocarpus and the Teleférico

One landmark visible from many parts of the city is the *Teleférico*, a castle-like building overlooking the town from a hill on the east side of Loja. Originally destined to be an aerial tram/tourist attraction, it was abandoned during construction when they ran out of funds.

The bottom half of this unfinished tram is in *Parque Colinar Pucará Podocarpus*, a city park with football fields, volleyball courts, a playground, and nice views of Loja, as well as a good restaurant (see more details in the next chapter). People often hike the trail to the unfinished buildings at the top of the hill to be rewarded with a great view of the city.

In the past, there were problems with thieves hiding along this trail, assaulting hikers and stealing their belongings. The police cracked down on the thieves, and reportedly this is no longer an issue. I have not heard any reports of recent incidents. While we were there in 2014, the graffiti and broken glass in the abandoned buildings gave me the impression that a rougher crowd probably still hung out up there after dark. During the day it seemed there was no problem, and we saw families with their children there. With the election of 2014, there were rumors that funding would return and the *Teleférico* would be completed.

As of our trip in 2017, the *Teleférico* remains unfinished. However, I observed with satisfaction that city workers had improved the trail to the upper half of the *Teleférico*, removed the trash and broken glass, and repainted and barred off the buildings to keep the troublemakers out. We also saw a night guard logbook on a table inside the locked building. Police officers now patrol the park 24 hours per day and there are also security cameras in place.

Parque "Daniel Álvarez Burneo"

Located in the southwestern part of the city in the Daniel Alvarez neighborhood, along the L-5 bus route, this smaller park has a little lake with a trail around it and a playground. It is another pleasant place to enjoy an easy walk, and, like the other parks, has been renovated and improved since our first visit in 2014.

Jardín Botánico Reinaldo Espinosa

This beautiful botanical garden has a $1.00 entrance fee (for foreigners, or 50 cents for locals), and it's totally worth it. Visiting hours are from 8 a.m. to 12:30 p.m. and 3 p.m. to 5:30 p.m. Monday through Friday, and from 1 p.m. to 5:30 p.m. on weekends. It is Ecuador's oldest public botanical garden (established in 1949) and has more than 800 species of plants organized into several different sections, including an orchid garden, medicinal plants, a vegetable garden where they grow indigenous foods, an orchard of Podocarpus trees (for which Podocarpus National Park was named), and more. We also saw several beautiful kinds of birds while strolling through the park. There's also a maze to entertain the kids. (And adults. Who are we kidding?)

Parque Eólico Villonaco

You'll probably notice the wind turbines on the ridge on the west side of town shortly after arriving in Loja.

The city's newest park is a popular tourist attraction, with visitors from different parts of Ecuador and abroad. A taxi to get up there will run $5-$8 or so.

Visitors to the park can learn about the project through park guides who give detailed talks about the wind turbines (in Spanish) and displays with signs and pictures about the project. The tour is free.

A major side benefit to visiting this park is the view. From the ridge, if it's a clear day, you'll have a beautiful view of the city of Loja on one side and the Catamayo valley on the other side. Be sure to dress for the wind, which can get cold!

Aside from all the larger city parks, Loja has many plazas, especially in the downtown area in front of the churches I described in the previous chapter. These are pretty areas to stroll around and people-watch from the benches.

Visit this book's companion website (access at **www.LilyAnnFouts.com/lojabonus**) to see photos and videos of the parks.

Hiking

Besides the city parks, Loja also has some great places to hike nearby. Some are organized parks, and others are trails that lead to remote homes in the mountains.

Parque Nacional Podocarpus

This national park provides wonderful hiking and bird watching opportunities. One entrance to the park is located only a few kilometers south of the city of Loja. The trails start about 5 kilometers up the dirt road from the entrance, which is next to the highway on the road to

Vilcabamba.

If you don't have a car, getting to the actual trailhead inside the park is tricky.

The cheapest option is to simply take the bus to the entrance and then hike 5 kilometers up the road to the trailhead.

The easiest option is to hire a taxi driver to take you all the way up, which from the southern end of Loja will likely cost $15 to $20. To get back to Loja after our hike we walked down the dirt road to the highway (a pleasant walk) and flagged down a bus. The other option is to call a taxi from the trailhead to come and get you (bring your cell phone or ask the ranger at the ranger station next to the trailhead if they could call one for you). So a taxi both ways would likely cost $30-$40.

Regardless of whether you drive, take a taxi or ride the bus, you'll need to stop at the entrance to the park and register (have your passport number handy), though admission is free.

Inside the park there are a couple of shorter, well-maintained trails from which you can birdwatch and enjoy the beautiful tropical plants. If you want a more strenuous hike there is a large loop which will take you up to the ridge and provide stunning views of the entire valley from Loja to Vilcabamba. For those seeking 2-3 day hiking expeditions you can also hire a guide to take you to the *Lagunas del Compadre*—a strenuous 8-hour hike. The best time of year for that hike is October and November. It is reportedly dangerous to make the trek during rainy season.

Parque Nacional Podocarpus has other entrances in Zamora and Vilcabamba, which I will cover in upcoming chapters.

Parque Universitario de Educación Ambiental y Recreación (PUEAR)

For the best maintained hiking trails right in town, head to the *Parque Universitario de Educación Ambiental y Recreación (PUEAR) "Francisco Vivar Castro."* This park, run by the *Universidad Nacional de Loja,* is on the southeast end of town across the road from the Botanical Gardens. They charge a $1.00 entrance fee ($0.50 for locals). Several kilometers of beautiful, well-maintained hiking trails wind through jungle and eucalyptus forest and to the ridge of a mountain overlooking Loja.

On our first trip to this park in 2014, Keith and I spent several hours hiking a loop that should have taken us less than two hours to complete, but the views and the flowers captivated our attention and we stopped every couple of minutes to take pictures.

A dog—probably belonging to one of the park employees—took it upon himself to become our guide and eagerly led us along the trail. Pets are not allowed in the park, but he insisted, and seemed quite familiar with the trails. I think he probably tags along with hikers on a regular basis to score free walks (and probably free food as well, considering how he would give us that begging puppy face each time one of us stopped and opened our packs). If you don't have a dog along, this park provides good birdwatching opportunities. There are several shelters along the trails, and we stopped in one of them for a picnic lunch.

We returned to this park in 2017 with visiting family members from the States, and still found it to be an excellent hiking spot! Everyone thoroughly enjoyed the views.

Sendero Ecológico Caxarumi: Loja-Vilcabamba
One of the newest developments in hiking opportunities is a trail that begins in *Parque La Tebaida* (see above) and extends all the way to Vilcabamba, a distance of approximately 40 kilometers! Instead of crossing the small bridge and returning to the park, as described in the section above, one may continue to walk the trails and country roads (watch for signs marking the official path) over the pass at the entrance to Podocarpus National Park, down the other side and onward, past small villages and fields still plowed with oxen. Although the trail officially goes all the way to Vilcabamba, we discovered that from San Pedro to Vilcabamba the arrows directed hikers to walk along the main highway, which we felt was unsafe since there is no path or sidewalk for pedestrians. If you hike this trail, I recommend stopping in Malacatos or San Pedro unless they re-route the end of the trail away from the highway. Watch carefully for the signs, especially in Malacatos and in the hills above Malacatos. We lost the trail and took a wrong turn a couple of times and had to double back to find it again.

The Teleférico
From the *Teleférico*, mentioned in the Parks section above, you can follow additional hiking trails through the hills on the east side of Loja. Descend the steep trail on the south side of the *Teleférico*, then follow it east into the woods and turn south again to follow the ridge. Along the way, you'll pass several interesting little sites, apparently used for military training. We descended the hill when we reached the big white cross. The steep trail down passes many smaller crosses, the 'stations of the cross.' In the

Catholic tradition, people re-enact Christ's crucifixion day each Easter with a walk past each of these stations to the cross at the top of the hill.

Exploration

One thing I love to do in a new area is simply to explore. Step onto a city bus (30 cents per ride) and see where it takes you. One day in 2014 we did this—we just hopped onto a random city bus to see where it would go. It took us toward the west side of town, climbing higher and higher up the side of the mountain toward the big wind turbines. We enjoyed spectacular views of Loja from the bus as we did this. From the end of the bus lines you'll often find a lot to explore on foot.

My personal recommendations:

1. Ride bus L-2 all the way north to the turnaround at Sauces Norte. Get off and keep hiking north. You'll pass a small Catholic church on the mountainside and keep going all the way to the top of the mountain (Cerro Zañe) and a white cross on top.

2. Ride bus L-7 all the way south to the turnaround at Barrio Punzara Grande. Climb up the hill toward the south and east, past a little lake (Laguna Aramara) to the cross at the top of that hill. For a more challenging hike, take the steep trail straight up the hill, and you can follow a trail for miles into the mountains. People live way back in there and the scenery is amazing.

3. Ride bus L-5 to Zamora-Huayco and get off at the end of that little canyon when the bus starts to loop back north (it's not a super clear turnaround point like some of the others, so watch for it). Follow the trail up the river.

(Note: I would skip the L-8 to Ciudad Victoria which looked like a rougher neighborhood.)

Sometimes you can find some great trails by simply walking beyond the paved roads at the edge of town. Travel up the dirt roads and you'll soon encounter trails, some of which lead to homes far up in the mountains which can only be reached on foot or with a pack animal. You may pass some residents ferrying items back and forth on their donkeys.

The first time we hiked beyond the edge of town, we took the L-2 *"Sauces Norte"* city bus all the way to the end of the line—the northernmost bus stop in the city. From there we could see a church way up on the hill, and began following the dirt roads toward it. After the church the road gradually turned to a trail and continued up the mountain, called *Cerro Zañe* (sometimes also spelled *Sañe*). Above the church we encountered an elderly indigenous lady who seemed curious about us. I suspect she lived in one of the mountain homes farther up the trail. We stopped and chatted with her for awhile before turning around to go home. We didn't have enough time to follow the trail to the end that day, but we returned with some friends on Christmas Eve, 2016, and hiked it all the way to a white cross on the summit. (See photos and videos on this book's companion website, which you can access at **http://www.LilyAnnFouts.com/lojabonus**.)

Another time we climbed out of Loja on the opposite end of town. Beyond the last neighborhood in the city, called *"Punzara Grande"* (at the southern end of the L-7 bus route) a dirt road winds onward into the mountains. Keith and I walked this road one day when a sociable woman named Mélida came out to chat with us. She asked us where we were from, where we lived, and what we were doing. She seemed happy that we had walked to her neighborhood and gave us a tour, showing us her husband's furniture shop and the view of the city beyond it.

"Everybody watches out for each other here," she said. "It's calm and quiet here and you won't have to worry about your safety."

When we told her we loved to hike, she smiled and pointed out a couple of trails leading out of her neighborhood into the mountains.

"That one goes up to a cross," she pointed eastward. "There is a pretty lake along the way." (We later learned that this small lake is called *Aramara*.) She told us that twice a year there is a great festival where her entire neighborhood makes a pilgrimage up to the cross.

She pointed to another trail that went steeply up the mountain next to her house. "That one goes for a long way into the mountains," she said. "I have never been all the way up it."

In the following days we made trips back to *Punzara Grande* and hiked up both trails, and found them both to be magnificent. The longer trail led up to homes tucked impossibly high into the mountains, and it's hard to believe that people still live in those homes and walk those trails regularly to get to and from town. In some places the trail was so stunningly beautiful that I told Keith it would be a national park if it were in the U.S.

In 2017, while Keith and I were riding all the bus lines in Loja (see Chapter Seven), who should step onto the bus in *Punzara Grande* but Mélida herself! She was excited to see us again and asked if we had hiked all the trails she had recommended to us. We told her we had, and she recommended exploring the area at the end of the L-12. We chatted until she reached her stop.

One time, our explorations almost got us into trouble. We followed a dirt road beyond the city limits up by the north side of the *Parque Pucará del Podocarpus.* As we hiked along we saw several yellow school vans drive by, so we assumed there must be a school somewhere ahead. Eventually we found a trail that led off the side of the road, so we decided to see where it went. Soon after, we encountered another dirt road, and on the other side of the road we saw what appeared to be a school building.

"Oh!" I said to Keith, "That must be the school the vans are driving to." Moments later, however, we saw a group of army men standing in formation, facing their sergeant, who had his back to us.

"Wait a minute…that's not a school—it's a military building!" I said to Keith.

One of the men in formation pointed at us and the sergeant turned around, and yelled to another man who saw us and came running toward us. Oops.

"What are you doing here?" he asked.

"We were out hiking," we responded, happy that we could at least speak Spanish and communicate with ease.

"Didn't you see the 'No trespassing' sign on the road?" he questioned.

"No, we followed a trail down the hill to this road—there were no signs the way we came," we answered truthfully.

"Where are you trying to go?" he asked us.

"We were exploring, but we wondered if the road would lead back into another part of town."

"Follow me; I will take you back to the road," he said. As we walked through the military base he pointed at various mountains and landmarks, telling us a few things about the area in a friendly conversational way. At the gate, he pointed down the road. "That's the way back into town," he said. "Have a great day."

Most of the time our expeditions led us into friendly interactions with the locals and discoveries of new and wonderful places. Stop along the way and grab a Popsicle from a neighborhood store. Chat with the locals. Ask them questions about their area and their families.

To see photos from some of our hikes and download a map that includes trails around Loja, visit the companion website. (Access at **http://www.LilyAnnFouts.com/lojabonus**.)

More Adventures

For more adventurous activities in the region, see if you can join a *LojAventura* trip.

LojAventura is a local adventure group which organizes monthly outings to natural attractions around the Province and sometimes has other hikes and smaller adventures closer to the city. Activities include hiking, rappelling, cycling, camping, backpacking, caving, and other adventures. Hang out with a bunch of locals doing something fun! The cost varies depending on the trip, but is always reasonable. Find out more on their website, **lojaventura.com**, and Facebook page, **www.facebook.com/lojaventura**.

Loja isn't a popular tourist destination yet, but it's a beautiful region with a lot of potential, and the city is working hard to boost tourism to the area.

Somehow, though, Loja's position off the beaten track makes it a more appealing place to make a home. There is enough going on in Loja and the surrounding towns to make it a pleasant place to live without having to deal with hordes of tourists (except during some of the festivals mentioned in the previous chapter). And for the adventurous traveler who likes hidden gems, Loja is a treasure.

In the next chapter, we'll cover places to eat and shop like a local in Loja!

CHAPTER TEN
Eating and Shopping

In addition to enjoying the activities Loja has to offer, you're going to want to find the best places to eat, and if you have a place to cook, you'll also want to shop for groceries and other household necessities. You may want to shop for some gifts or souvenirs for family members back home, too. This chapter is all about eating and shopping in Loja. Let's dive in!

Eating
I won't be delving into a long discussion of Ecuadorian

cuisine in this book—as a vegetarian I don't feel entirely qualified to comment on the full range of foods available—but I will mention that if Mexico is your only experience with Latin America, you may be surprised to discover that the food of Ecuador (and other Latin American countries) is almost nothing like Mexican food. I did not encounter spicy food in Loja other than bottles of hot sauce that you could sprinkle on the food if you wished. While it may not be as exciting as Mexican cuisine, Ecuadorian food is filling, nutritious, and delicious.

Typical Ecuadorian lunches and dinners can easily be found in restaurants all over town for about $2.50 per plate. These simple but filling meals typically start with a bowl of soup at lunch time (but not at supper time), and include a drink and a generous plate filled with plain rice, fried plantain and/or potatoes, a salad of some sort, and some sort of legume (beans, peas, or lentils) and a meat option. We are vegetarians, so substituting the meat with a couple of eggs was never a problem, and often they actually reduced the price for us since eggs are cheaper than meat.

You'll have a lot more options if you're a meat eater (the most popular meat seemed to be chicken), especially if you're an adventurous eater (i.e., willing to eat certain parts of the meat that may not be common to eat where you come from), but as vegetarians a few of the usual things we found to eat (in addition to the traditional plate described above) included:

- *humitas* (similar to Mexican tamales, without a meat filling; made with corn and cheese and steamed in corn husks)
- *quimbolitos* (similar to humitas, but sweet.

Made with wheat and/or corn flour, raisins mixed in, and steamed in large green leaves)
- *bolón de verde con queso* (fried balls of plantain with cheese)
- *empanadas* (fried breads usually filled with cheese or chicken)
- *empanadas de verde* (as above, except mashed plantain instead of bread dough)
- *empanadas de yuca* (as above, except made with yuca flour—or a mixture of yuca and wheat flour)
- *tortillas* (thick and very different from Mexican tortillas, sometimes with cheese in them)
- *tostadas* (grilled cheese sandwiches—not the Mexican tostadas you may be used to)
- *chifles* (plantain chips)

Ecuadorian tamales almost always come filled with chicken or pork, but we got to know one one shop owner and asked if later that week she could make us a dozen tamales filled with cheese instead. She happily did so, and sold them to us at the same cost as her regular tamales. They were delicious!

By the way, cheese in Ecuador is different from most common cheeses in the U.S. It is a fresh, crumbly cheese. There are two main varieties—*queso* and *quesillo*—and neither of them are like cheddar, American, mozzarella or Swiss cheese. They are more like the *queso fresco* from Mexico. *Quesillo* melts easily and is a common ingredient in soups, while *queso* is good for grilling.

It's also easy to find fresh fruit juices and smoothies (*jugos* and *batidos*) in many places.

Bakeries are common throughout the city if you enjoy

fresh breads and pastries at a low price.

Loja does have some local specialties. My favorite was a creamy white soup made from green bananas or green plantains called *repe blanco* or *repe lojano*. We found it up by *Parque Pucará* near the *Teleférico* on the east side of town, in a restaurant also called *Pucará de Podocarpus*.

Fancier restaurants with a full menu to choose from will cost you more than the common restaurants found all over—especially if they offer foods other than Ecuadorian options. Some of the pizza places actually cost as much or more than pizza in the U.S.! Loja has some upscale restaurants, but not many.

The following restaurants are ones we visited and enjoyed ourselves, and/or were highly recommended to us by several locals:

- *Mama Lola,* highly recommended for its traditional dishes from Loja. On Av. Salvador Bustamante Celi y Santa Rosa (on the corner, Sector El Valle). **www.facebook.com/mamalolarestaurante**
- *Pucará del Podocarpus*, another great place for traditional local cuisine. This restaurant also offers one of the best views of the city and was recently renovated! On Calle Cesar Vallejo, next to *Parque Colinar Pucará.*
- *Tamal Lojano*, another highly recommended café with lots of local specialties. On 18 de Noviembre and Imbabura in front of P*arque Bolívar,* with another branch on 24 de Mayo between Mercadillo and Azuay. **http://tamallojano.com**.
- *Toro Rojo Steakhouse*, recommended by several local friends. Near the intersection of Juan José Peña and Mercadillo.

- *Zarza Brewing Co.*, Loja's first craft brewery, owned by a Texan/Ecuadorian couple. Popular with both locals and expats. Incredible Tex-Mex food and craft beers. On the corner of Esmeraldas and Pto. Bolivar in El Valle.
  www.zarzabrewing.com
- *Riscomar,* an eatery with seafood and more, recommended by several locals. Near the intersection of 24 de Mayo and Rocafuerte.
  www.riscomarloja.com.
- *El Torito*, good, inexpensive Mexican food with several vegetarian options. Nice location right next to the tower in Plaza San Sebastian. Try to get a table overlooking the plaza on the second floor! Great place to eat right before enjoying *Jueves Culturales*.
  www.facebook.com/ElToritoMexicanBarGrill
- *Restaurant Balcón de la Plaza*, another restaurant in Plaza San Sebastian, on the second floor of a building on Bolívar directly across the street (to the west) from the church steps. This is another place to get good local food for cheap, and have a nice view of the plaza while you eat. We ate there for lunch with our visiting family members and had typical lunch of soup, a drink, and a full plate of food for less than $3 each. They even included a small dessert, which is unusual!
- *Tutto Freddo* and *Nice Cream* (Two downtown locations, same company. Tutto Freddo is at Bolívar and 10 de Agosto close to the Plaza Central; Nice Cream is at Bolívar and Mercadillo in Plaza San Sebastian.) This is the *best* ice cream in Loja according to every single local I asked.

www.tuttofreddo.ec

For more links to these restaurants, visit the companion website. (Access at **www.LilyAnnFouts.com/lojabonus**.)

Grocery Shopping

The cheapest way to eat is to buy groceries and cook your own meals. If you have access to a kitchen and have the inclination to cook (which could happen after a few days if you're vegetarian and like some variety in your diet like we do), get ready to go shopping!

If you just need to pick up a few small things—maybe some cooking oil, milk, or a couple of onions—within a few blocks of anywhere you'll probably find a little neighborhood *tienda* (store) selling a lot of snacks and basic pantry foods, and possibly a little produce or bakery goods. These are extremely convenient when you forget something and don't have the time or inclination to go all the way to a major market or grocery store, but not practical or economical for a large-scale shopping trip.

Supermarket Chains

The stores where most North Americans and Europeans will feel at ease are the Supermaxi, which is located in a shopping center in the south part of town, and Gran AKI, across from Mercado Mayorista near the *Puerta de la Ciudad*. Any taxi driver will know exactly where to go if you just say "Supermaxi" or "Gran AKI."

Both Gran AKI and Supermaxi are grocery store chains much like any grocery store chain you shop in at home—you push a shopping cart through the aisles selecting what you want to buy. All prices are clearly marked. Then you pay for it at a modern checkout counter when you're done. It hardly gets more familiar than that. One slightly different aspect is that if you come into the store with a large backpack or bag, a security person there will check it in and store it for you (at Supermaxi) or you store it in a locker (at Gran AKI) and then you can pick it back up before you leave.

Large, clean and modern, Supermaxi and Gran AKI have pretty much all the things you'd expect—food, personal care products, cleaning products, kitchen gadgets, and so on. The selection is decent—though not as hugely varied as what people are used to coming from the U.S. (in other words, you won't encounter 67 different kinds of toothpaste). Gran AKI also carries furniture, electronics, and clothing in addition to the regular grocery store items, similar to a Walmart Supercenter.

Another chain with smaller but similar stores is TÍA, with locations downtown and in the *El Valle* shopping mall, and Zerimar, near the *Puerta de la Ciudad*.

On the downside, these stores are often among the more expensive places to buy food, so if you want to shop like a local I recommend reserving them for buying specialty items you can't find at the neighborhood *mercados*. Also, chain stores are boring.

Mercados

There are a few major *mercados* that open daily in Loja. They open early and close by mid-afternoon, so do your shopping in the morning! These are the main mercados in Loja:

- **Mercado Mayorista**, north of downtown near the *Puerta de la Ciudad* and across the street from Gran AKI. You'll be able to find produce, meats,

eggs, cheese, etc., as well as prepared food and household items in this market and the stores on the streets surrounding it.
- The biggest and busiest *mercado*—**Mercado Centro Comercial Loja**—is located downtown, with all produce, meats, cheese and flowers for sale on the lower level and clothing, shoes, accessories, paper products, hair salons/barber shops and more on the top floor. There's also a "food court" area with juice and food vendors on the top floor—a great place to grab a meal next to the locals for cheaper than pretty much anywhere else. Many additional shops line the streets surrounding the *mercado*.
- Also downtown is the **Mercado "San Sebastian"**—smaller, but with all the basics—produce, meats, etc. You'll find it in the *Plaza San Sebastian*.
- A still smaller *mercado*—**Mercado "La Tebaida"**—is located across the river from the Supermaxi on the south side of town. This was the *mercado* closest to where we lived during both of our stays in Loja. We sometimes shopped there during the week if we needed something, but like most of the people living in Loja, we did the majority of our shopping on Saturday, when the open air market opened up on the streets surrounding this *mercado*.

Weekly Open-Air Markets

The open air markets, or *ferias libres* in Spanish, happen once a week—most on Saturday or Sunday—and that is where you will find the best deals on groceries. We usually fill up our shopping bags with as much as two of us can carry, which is plenty of food for the next week, and spend around $20 to $40, depending on what we get. Note that these open-air markets open early in the morning and close up by early afternoon, so don't put your shopping trip off for later in the day! You'll find a *feria libre* in one of the following neighborhoods:

On Saturdays:
- La Pradera
- La Tebaida (across the river from Supermaxi)
- In Jipiro

On Sundays:
- San Sebastián (downtown, starting from Plaza San Sebastian)
- Época
- La Banda
- Agroecológica (the last Sunday of each month)

On Fridays:
- Esteban Godoy
- Héroes del Cenepa

On Tuesdays:
- Celi Román

Most expats I talked to seem to like the *feria libre* of San Sebastian the best, but Keith and I liked the one in our neighborhood, La Tebaida. All are crowded, so be prepared. It's like your farmer's market back home, times 1,000.

While grocery shopping in the U.S. is a dull and boring experience, I find shopping in the outdoor market genuinely enjoyable in Ecuador. We actually looked forward to it every week! It's a vibrant place, full of activity—and you never know what you'll find. James, an expat living in Loja, described it as a "scavenger hunt"— sometimes you'll find something and it may be six months before you see it again, depending on the growing seasons.

When you return week after week, you begin to recognize the vendors. I love fresh flowers, and in Ecuador they are so cheap (usually only a dollar or two for a nice bouquet, depending on the type of flowers) that I developed the habit of buying a new bouquet from one particular lady each week. When she noticed that I kept coming back to buy from her, she began giving me extra flowers for free with the bouquets I bought.

Another experience I enjoyed about grocery shopping in Loja was the huge variety of new and exotic fruits and vegetables that I had never seen before. Literally every week that we went to the market, there was some new kind of fruit or vegetable that I had never seen—not even during my childhood in Mexico. It made for a great excuse to talk to the vendors, asking them questions about what it was, what it tasted like, the best way to prepare it, and then always buying some to take home and try.

I wouldn't be performing my duty as a vegetarian if I didn't mention the health food store in Loja. It's nowhere as big as the chain health food stores we're used to in the U.S., but they have a nice selection of veggie meats, supplements, good whole wheat bread and more. It's called *Alivinatu* and it's about half a block East of the Southeast corner of the *Parque Central,* on *10 de Agosto* between *Olmedo* and *Bernardo Valdivieso* streets. They also have a café where they serve good vegetarian food, though it is more expensive.

Finding the Best Deals

One cultural difference between Mexico and Ecuador that surprised me was the attitude toward haggling. While growing up in Mexico, I learned the friendly banter between seller and shopper. It went something like this:

Shopper: How much for these three tomatoes?
Seller: Three for a dollar!
Shopper: That's way too much. I'll pay you 30 cents!
Seller: I'll give them to you for 60 cents.
Shopper: Forty.
Seller: Fifty.
Shopper: Okay.

I assumed Ecuador would be the same way, and I fear I offended a few sellers on our first foray to the *mercado*. They would quote me a price, which truthfully seemed pretty good to me, but I assumed they were quoting me a high price so that I would bargain them down. I would throw back a lower price and they would look offended. *"No sale"* (roughly translated it means 'I can't make a profit at that ridiculously low price'), they would say shaking their heads, and wave me away.

I decided to be quiet for a few minutes and see what they were charging the locals. To my surprise and delight, I noticed that the locals were being quoted the same prices that we were. I also noticed that they weren't haggling. The fact that locals usually treated us equally even though we were obviously foreigners was one thing that I came to love about Loja. I couldn't say the same for the areas with a high percentage of expats.

There are still occasionally some vendors who will try to extract a higher price from us. It was rare, but to guard against this I developed the habit of asking the price of something from several different vendors to learn what the fair price was, or I would listen to what they were quoting the locals. Then I would either go to the vendor who quoted the best price, or tell the vendor I was speaking to what the vendor a few stalls down was selling the same item for, and they usually agreed to give me the same price as the other vendor. Sometimes if you ask a price and then begin to walk away, the vendor will call after you and lower the price to encourage you to come back and buy.

Other Shopping

For other needs, such as clothing, electronics, gifts, souvenirs, household appliances, and furniture, there are a number of options to choose from in Loja. For large and expensive items, some people find it cheaper to buy in Cuenca and transport the items to Loja, so it may be worth shopping around.

Malls

Loja has two malls: *El Valle* and the new *Mall "Don Daniel,"* in addition to a few strip malls around town (for example, next to Supermaxi and next to Gran AKI) and several collections of shops in the downtown area.

El Valle contains a food court, an arcade, and the city's only movie theater on the top floor (**www.cinemasloja.com**). The movies are usually dubbed in Spanish. The mall has several other stores, including the TÍA grocery store on the first floor. We noticed a few vacant shops inside this mall. It feels like it might be in decline, possibly due to competition from the new mall across town.

Mall "Don Daniel" opened recently and is a block north of the Supermaxi shopping area. There are a number of typical mall shops inside selling clothing, housewares, shoes (including a Payless ShoeSource), and a food court on the top floor. According to several local friends, the Wifi in Mall Don Daniel is also very good, though I never used it myself.

Gifts and Souvenirs

If you're looking from some local souvenirs for yourself or your family, the most popular spot to look is on *Calle Lourdes*, a narrow, cobble-stoned east-west street located one block south of *Plaza San Sebastian* and heading west. This quaint little street has several shops selling local and national arts and crafts, pottery, etc.

Another crafts shop can be found on the east side of *Calle Bolívar*, just south of *10 de Agosto*, near the *Parque Central*.

Also, every Sunday a collection of arts and crafts vendors congregates in the *Parque Central*. You can find souvenirs, candy, and ice cream there. One vendor, Francisco Cuenca, has some nice local pottery, or *cerámica Lojana*. If you're not around to see it on Sunday, you can find him at his shop the rest of the week at *Barrio Borja, calle Cucuta y Barquisimeto*.

For a personalized and unique souvenir, contact Diego Díaz for a custom-made carved rock. He will hand-carve anything you want into a river rock (sizes vary from palm-sized to dinner plate-sized). He carved a beautiful clock for Keith and me, with images of us at the top of a mountain.

To see pictures of Diego's rock carvings and to contact him, visit his Facebook page at **http://bit.ly/rumiloja** or call 98 527 0354 (Spanish only).

Note on Prices in Ecuador

For non-food needs, such as clothing, electronics, furniture and household items, there is a range of options and prices in Loja. Anything that is imported—even cheap made-in-China stuff—will be considerably more expensive than what you are used to in the U.S. Recently a trade agreement was signed between Ecuador and Europe, so some prices will begin to drop in the coming years. Nevertheless, some wealthier Ecuadorians actually fly to the U.S. to save money on their high-end shopping.

While food in Ecuador is extremely inexpensive, shoes and clothing can cost more, especially if it is imported and/or high quality. Also, if you aren't a typical Ecuadorian size (i.e. smaller than most people in the U.S.), it may be harder to find clothes that fit. I have a hard enough time in the U.S. finding pants that fit my long legs. It would be much harder in Ecuador, where the women are, on average, nine inches shorter than I am. You might consider shopping for clothes before going to Ecuador.

Expect to pay higher than U.S. prices for virtually all electronics. Electronics made in Ecuador may be cheaper, but also lower quality. If you want a smartphone, a laptop, a camera, etc, try to bring those with you from the U.S. (Check customs/import laws, though—some of these items may be subject to tax, especially if you bring more than one per person into Ecuador.)

For smaller household items, again the price will depend on whether the item is Ecuadorian made and the level of quality. Some expats recommend bringing your own set of sheets since nice sheets can be hard to find and/or expensive in Ecuador. Once you become a legal resident of Ecuador, you will be allowed to ship a container of your things from the U.S., duty-free.

Depending on what you want, it may or may not be worth it to do so, but if you do then that would be a great opportunity to stock up on clothing, high quality small and large appliances, high quality cookware, and good bedding and towels, if these things are important to you. Personally, I'm not sure I would bother with the expense of shipping a container, but everybody is different.

An excellent source of information for moving to Ecuador, including recommended shipping companies and much more detailed information about the process, can be found in a book called *Becoming an Expat: Ecuador* by Shannon Enete. To order it on Amazon visit this link: **http://amzn.to/1BRArr1**

I highly recommend that book as a supplement to the information in this book about Loja, since it gives a comprehensive overview of the process of moving to Ecuador and establishing residency.

Services

Shopping for services? In general, labor is cheap, so if you need something made or repaired, Ecuador is a great place to go!

General Services

Haircuts are around $2 - $3, or $4 - $5 if you have it styled, too.

If you have a hole in your clothes and need a seamstress, you'll pay a dollar or two for the job. Keith took his day pack in for a repair since the straps were coming loose and a hole was forming in the bottom. He had it fixed for less than $2.00. We came back with a pile of mending in 2017 and had five items repaired for $8.00.

If you don't have laundry facilities where you're

staying, you can take a load to a laundromat and have it washed, dried, and folded for you for a few cents per pound of clothing (one expat recently reported paying $0.36 per pound). You might want to do this anyway just to save time!

Vehicle maintenance, car washing and detailing, custom furniture, furniture repair, appliance repair, handymen…just about any service you can think of will be much cheaper in Ecuador than it is in the US.

Medical and Dental Care

Dentistry and medical services are much less, too. As with medical and dental services anywhere, there are good doctors and there are bad doctors. Try to find people who have been there before and can give a recommendation, and if possible try to set up a consultation to see if you're comfortable with the health care professional. Each person is different and may feel comfortable with different health care providers.

A common question people ask about Loja is, how good is the medical care there? Most expats I have spoken with have been pleased with their level of care. For example, the Spanish couple in our apartment building became pregnant with their first baby while they lived in Ecuador. They went in for regular checkups and ultrasounds, and when I asked them about their experience they told me they were impressed the care they received, saying it was as good as any care they had received in Spain. They said the facilities were modern and the staff seemed competent and attentive. Their baby was born in Loja.

An American expat told me of problems he had with skin cancer. He received excellent treatment which cleared up most of his skin. He had surgery to remove the remaining cancer and everything was successful. Healthcare costs are low enough that he is self-insured.

Another expat related via a Facebook post that she had once (a few years ago) had an accident after which she was hospitalized in Loja with broken ribs, punctured lung, and concussion. She'd had a 3-night/4-day stay in a massive private room with satellite TV and phone, CAT scan, x-rays, chest tube to re-inflate lung, good doctors and nurses and all her medications after hospitalization, all for less than $800.

During our most recent trip to Loja, I moved my hips a little too enthusiastically during dance class and managed to injure myself. I had already been having problems with my hip off and on for the previous year and had been seeing a chiropractor in the US about it. The pain worsened throughout the evening and kept me awake most of the night. By the next day I couldn't even lift my leg to put my sock on.

We visited a local friend and I asked her where I should go. She recommended Doctora Patricia Orellana who has an office on Calle Lourdes—the same street with all the souvenir shops. The place is a spa called *"Zait Sebastian"* and they specialize in all manner of physical therapy, massage, and more. I set up an appointment for the next day and limped in.

I received a consultation, wonderful massage complete with hot compresses to relax the muscles, and an injection of mild anesthetics (neural therapy, a common method of treatment in Europe and South America but somewhat controversial in the US) from the doctor. She also sent me home with a special type of ointment to rub onto the affected area twice a day for the next couple of weeks.

My hip didn't feel better immediately, but my back felt great from the massage. By the next day my hip felt 99% better, literally almost back to normal. I followed the doctor's advice by using the ointment every day and avoiding strenuous hikes and dancing for the next several days, even though my hip felt fine. I haven't had problems with it since. The total cost for all treatment and medications was $30.

Another expat I know went in for a podiatry treatment after having problems with his feet and described the feeling when he left as "walking on clouds." If you need or want a massage or any type of physical therapy, I recommend this place. The address is Lourdes 14-49 entre Bolívar y Sucre. Phone: 07 257 0830 or 099 284 7744. Or email at zaitsebastianspa@gmail.com.
www.facebook.com/zait.sebastianspa

The cost of medical care in Ecuador is low enough that Keith and I did not bother to buy traveler's insurance for our trips, like we usually do. I recommend you assess the situation to determine whether that is the best decision for you, but in our case we felt that we would be able to handle a medical expense out of pocket in Ecuador for most problems we might have while there. Many visitors and expats carry medical evacuation and/or catastrophic insurance for accidents or major needs, but pay everything else out of pocket.

For medical needs in Loja, I've seen *Clínica San Augustín* recommended most often. They are a hospital and have a full lab, emergency room, and doctors for many specialties. The hospital is located at *18 de Noviembre 10-72 and Azuay* **http://hospitalclinicasanagustin.com**.

There are several dentists whom I have seen recommended several times each by expats in Loja. They are:
- *Dr. Claudio Campoverde*, reportedly the high-end dentist whom Lojanos with money visit. They say he is diligent with continuing education, attending dental workshops in the US and Brazil, speaks decent English, and does high-quality work with high-quality equipment. He charges $40 for a cleaning with ultra-sound. The office is located at Av. Emiliano Ortega 07-65 and 10 de Agosto. Phone: (07) 2 578170.
- *Oralcorp.* Dr. Luis y Dra. Vanessa reportedly speak English. They even have an English version of their website! The office is at Sucre 21-26 and Catamayo, behind the Supermaxi. Contact at info@oralcorp.com.ec or at one of these phone numbers: 072582139 - 0998870000 - 0992717174 - 0995640728. **www.oralcorp.com/site**
- *Dra. Teresa Campaña Y.,* who conducted her dentistry residency in the U.S. The dental office, "Family Dental Care," is located at *Jose Felix de Valdivieso 15-22* between *Sucre* and *18 de Noviembre.* Phone number: 07 2586355. familydentalcareloja@yahoo.com.

Despite the positive stories I have heard about medical care in Loja, I have also heard that the level of care can vary greatly depending on whether you go to a public hospital or a private one. Everyone in Ecuador is guaranteed free medical care at public hospitals, but these are often overcrowded and under-equipped.

For better care, many Ecuadorians (and other legal

residents of Ecuador) pay into the country's public health care program, which gives them access to IESS (IESS stands for *Instituto Ecuatoriano de Seguridad Social,* or Ecuadorian Institute of Social Security) facilities.

For the very best care with the highest standards and best equipment, those who can afford it go to private medical facilities. The cost of these facilities is higher than many locals can afford, but still much cheaper than anything we pay in the United States.

I have also heard of expats who have had to leave Loja due to the limited availability of medical services there. It sounds to me like most smaller and routine medical needs could be taken care of in Loja, but if you have a serious health concern or major illness, you may need to choose a larger city or even consider staying in your home country.

For more information and any new up-to-date recommendations for medical, dental or other services in Loja, check the companion website. (Access at **www.LilyAnnFouts.com/lojabonus**.)

Our next topic is finding and setting up a home in Loja. In the next chapter we'll talk about finding a long-term apartment, getting your utilities hooked up, and locating furniture and appliances.

CHAPTER ELEVEN
Setting Up House

I hoped that when we arrived in Loja for our first visit and could meet people in person, that the house hunting process would become easier, because I couldn't find much online. The morning after our arrival, we began walking around the town and asking people if they knew of any furnished apartments for rent. Most had no idea where we could even begin to look for such a thing. A few recommended looking in the newspaper classifieds, but we didn't find much there—and everything we did find was unfurnished.

In the afternoon we returned to our hotel room, defeated. An idea struck. I plopped down with my laptop and searched the Airbnb site. Sure enough, there was one nice looking furnished apartment building in Loja. It was called *"Apartamentos del Rio."* Unfortunately, they wanted $750 per month, which was quite a lot more than we had planned to spend. I figured if we could find the apartment managers in person, we would be able to negotiate a better rate.

I punched *"Apartamentos del Rio, Loja, Ecuador"* into the search engine and found them listed on a few other sites. Piecing together the information that I found, I was able to determine the approximate location of the apartments. We hailed a taxi to the neighborhood and started asking around. Finally, someone pointed us toward the hotel, *Jardines del Rio*, and I guessed that due to the similar names, the owners of the hotel might also be the owners of the apartments.

As we came up the stairs into *Jardines del Rio*, we met Cristian, the oldest son of the family who managed the hotel and, yes, the apartments! Cristian welcomed us in and told us about the apartments, and wrote down the price as he spoke. Month-to-month, $650. If we were willing to sign a one year lease, the apartments would be $450 per month. We asked about a two month lease. It would be $600 per month. This was still a couple hundred more than we had hoped to pay, but it did include the water and electric bills and it seemed our options were limited. As far as we could tell, this might be the only place in the city offering furnished short-term rentals.

The next morning we met Cristian at the hotel and together we went to tour the brand new apartment building. These were not the same apartments as in the pictures on Airbnb, but they were lovely. They were in the process of furnishing the units and installing the stoves and water heaters, and Cristian assured us that they would be ready by Wednesday. Meanwhile, he said, we could stay at the same rate in a room in their hotel until the apartment was ready. We loved the views from the apartment building, across the road from *Parque La Tebaida*, one of the biggest parks in town. From the rooftop terrace we could see the mountains surrounding the town, too.

 We decided to go for it. We picked the apartment at the top of the building (for the best views and most privacy) and signed the two-month lease. For the next two months, luxury would be ours! On Saturday the 25th of January we moved our stuff into the hotel room, which was beautiful and even had a loft with another bed in case we had any visitors. We had negotiated for them to include a good, hot breakfast for us while we were there, too.

 Each morning we enjoyed our jam and bread, scrambled eggs, milk and coffee, and freshly made fruit juice and while counting down the days until we would have our own place with our own kitchen. On Monday night, Iván, the father of the family, met us as we came back to the hotel after sightseeing.

 "I have a beautiful apartment here, in the back of the hotel, that just became available!" he said. "It has three bedrooms instead of two, and it comes with a washing machine; it's all ready for you to move into right now if you wish! Would you like to see it? No pressure if you'd still rather have the other place!"

 We took a look at it, but I didn't care for it. It was old and dark, and faced a walled-in courtyard instead of the beautiful mountains. To get to it, we would have to walk through the hotel every day. I realized then that our apartment would not be ready by Wednesday. Keith and I decided we still wanted the new apartments, but told Iván that we would be willing to move to the third floor rather than the fourth floor unit we had originally chosen, because we knew the third floor unit was closer to being done. I asked if our move-in date was still on track for Wednesday.

"No, we've had a delay getting the stoves and hot water heaters installed," he explained apologetically. "But for sure by Thursday or Friday it will be done! I want to make sure everything is done right before we hand over the apartment. Oh, by the way, we need you to pay another $600."

"But we already paid the first month's rent..." I said.

"For the deposit! And so we can get the furniture for the apartment." Sigh. Yep, we're in Latin America.

"If we give you the $600 you will give us a receipt for the 2nd month's rent, and we will owe nothing more for the two months we live there, right?"

"Yes, yes, of course!" he agreed.

I asked Iván to put the hand-over date in writing on the contract, along with the change from the fourth floor unit to the third floor. He obliged. "The apartment will be handed over on the 31st of January," he wrote.

Tuesday we paid our 2nd month of rent, and received our corresponding receipt.

Tuesday night we returned from our explorations and met Iván on the stairwell on the way to our room.

"Surprise!" he said, beaming. "Your apartment is almost ready! You will be able to move in tomorrow morning! We are putting the final touches on it now."

I was pleasantly surprised. "That's wonderful news!" I

said. So after everything, the apartment would be ready on Wednesday after all, as originally promised! I should have known better.

The next morning after breakfast Keith and I happily packed up our luggage and carried it down to the lobby. Moments later, an apologetic Iván came out to meet us. "Oh, I am so sorry," he said. "The apartment is still not ready yet. I didn't realize, they still haven't finished the stove. I am so embarrassed!" He helped us carry our luggage back up to our room.

Thursday, we asked the mother of the family, Magdalena, how the apartment was coming along. "Almost done!" she said. "I just took the curtains in today to have them taken up; they were dragging on the ground. They should be finished by tomorrow."

The official hand-off day rolled around: Friday, January 31st. Keith and I packed our bags and went for a hike, then came back to the hotel and waited. Finally, Cristian came for us. "Are you ready?" he asked? "Very ready!" I replied. The hotel was beautifully decorated and the family and staff pleasant, but our room was old with a crumbly wood floor, and the shower came with an electric shower head (common in Latin America) which would flip on and off with the changing water pressure, making showers a difficult ordeal. We were ready for our brand new place, and a kitchen to cook our own food (as I alluded to in Chapter Ten, selection for vegetarians in most of the local restaurants was limited).

Cristian helped us carry our luggage over to the new apartment, where Magdalena was hanging a curtain. We came in and looked around. The apartment was tastefully furnished, but some of the furniture was older (the table rocked on squeaky metal legs and had a stained top and chairs, for example).

"Where's the stove?" I asked, noting a gaping hole in the countertop.

"Oh, they haven't come to install them yet; they will be here on Monday–Tuesday at the latest," said Magdalena. Cristian came in a few minutes later packing a stand-alone stove, and then brought in a gas cylinder and hooked it up.

"You can cook on this over the weekend until we install the permanent stove," they told us.

Well, at least we had a stove. And a fridge. The house came with all the basic dishes we would need, beds with bedding (although our full size bed had a twin-size flat sheet on it), a TV, and lamps.

But then there were some other little details, like no curtains on the windows facing the apartment across from us. No frying pan. No cutting board. No broom or mop. No towels. No rack to hang towels in the bathroom. No toilet paper holder, either.

The nozzle for the cold water barely allowed any cold water to flow, and the water burned me during my first shower. The tub, installed slightly askew, encouraged water to pour out onto the floor and run toward the hardwood bedroom floors. Keith hurled our laundry onto the floor to stop the flow and installed a little dam made of duct tape to reroute the water into the tub and down the drain.

Over the next day I wrote down a list of things we needed and took them to Cristian at the hotel. "No problem, no problem," he said in his usual agreeable way. " *Mañana* we will bring you all this stuff."

Tomorrow. *Mañana*. The word doesn't actually mean tomorrow. In Latin America, *mañana* means "at some point in the indefinite future, after we have spent some time with our families, and if we get around to it." Some of it they got around to. Some of it they didn't. The stove took over a month. The frying pan and towels came right away. The towel rack and toilet paper holder never happened, and neither did the cold water in the shower ever get fixed; we had to turn down the temperature on the hot water heater instead. The little duct tape dam was still in place when we moved out.

On February 10, I wrote in my journal: "This evening we heard some commotion upstairs and went up, thinking the landlords were doing a bit of work." (Whenever we heard the landlords we often went out to request something that we were still waiting on...) "Nope–it was just our neighbors installing a dish for satellite TV. They, being European, and we, of the U.S., have all been frustrated with the cultural differences with the landlords when it comes to accomplishing things. The downside to being the first occupants of this brand new apartment building is that we're the first ones to discover what doesn't work, what's missing, and what's wrong...and our landlords seem to lack the inclination and/or money to fix anything, even though we are assured with lots of smiles that it will be taken care of "right away." This weekend! Monday, for sure! Tuesday, at the very latest! On and on it goes. We have a hole in our counter which is meant for a stove which was to be installed two days after we moved in. The deadline is now over a week past... Still, it's a great apartment. We have a back-up stove for the moment and we're comfortable. Patience is key in Latin America."

Overall, we were happy and comfortable in our apartment in Loja, but all the friends we met there agreed we were paying a luxury price for a non-luxury apartment.

Our neighbors within the apartment building had

stories of their own to share. One spent her first three days without hot water. Another had specifically asked the landlords not to come in until she home (she had a dog and didn't want her getting out), and when she returned home she found the door ajar and the landlords working inside. In our periodic gatherings with the neighbors in our building, there were always more stories going around. We were a multi-national bunch, with us from the States, another couple from Spain, one woman from Venezuela, and another originally from Ecuador but who had lived for many years in France.

The cultural differences between Latin America and Europe and North America took some by surprise. The concept of privacy is totally different. When we asked for curtains between us and the other apartment, their response was "Oh, nobody is living over there yet, so we'll just put something up before anyone moves in." The fact that they themselves were often over there working on the apartment–sometimes late at night–didn't seem to occur to them as an issue. They would always wave cheerfully through the windows.

On the evening before our departure, we invited all of our neighbors for tea/coffee and cookies, and a giveaway extravaganza. Because our landlords failed to provide many basic household items, we had purchased a few things to get us by, but we felt our neighbors could probably use them more than the landlords. We sat around and chatted for awhile and Keith and I encouraged our neighbors to take what they wanted from the pile we had made on the table.

They looked at the items shyly, sheepishly taking a small thing or two each. "Take everything!" we encouraged them. "Whatever you don't take stays here and the landlords will get to keep it." Their expressions changed from a look of shyness to a look of, "Hell, no!" Moments later, everything was gone.

Iván, Magdalena, Cristian and his siblings are all pleasant people—I liked all of them—but their way of life is different from what many North Americans or Europeans may be accustomed to. For me, the experience refreshed my memory–having grown up in Mexico it was a bit like coming home. Still, we all agreed that the apartments were too expensive for the level of quality and service we received in return, and we all said we'd be looking at other options if we had it to do over again. At least the landlords lived up to their promise and never asked us for more money! Overall I found the Ecuadorians to be overwhelmingly fair and honest and generous with us.

Keith and I made several new friends who said they could help us in the house hunt the next time we went down. Still, it is Ecuador. It is Latin America. I expect we will always have different ideas of privacy, different expectations for how fast things should be done or how well things should work. This is how it is. Take a deep breath and accept that things will be different. Patience is key!

Every culture has its pros and cons. I appreciate many things about Latin America's culture and overall I feel more at home there than I do in the U.S. Learn to appreciate the lovely people, the importance of family, and the lack of importance of schedules. There is common phrase in Ecuador: *Ama la vida.* Love life. Take it to heart!

Tips and Resources for House Hunting

After finding our apartment, I have since discovered some other resources for finding a house in Loja. For rentals of a few months or less, there are now many more options listed on Airbnb than there were in 2014.

For longer-term rentals of unfurnished homes or to look for property to buy, OLX seems to be the "Craigslist" of Ecuador—with everything from apartments to cars to furniture for sale.

http://ciudadloja.olx.com.ec

Some other good classifieds sites include:
- **http://loja.doplim.ec/**
- **http://casas.trovit.com.ec/**
- **The FB group, "Southern Ecuador Property (Buy/Sell/Rent)"**
- **The FB group, "Arriendos, ventas de locales, casas, terrenos en Loja"**

For more links, see the companion website. Access at **www.LilyAnnFouts.com/lojabonus**.

I'd advise against arranging a long-term rental before arriving in Loja. Many apartments are advertised via signs in the window, so a good way to go about finding a long-term place to rent at a decent price would be to decide which part of town you like best, then simply walk around that neighborhood and look for signs saying something like '*Se arrienda*,' '*Arriendo Departamento*,' and arrange to look at the place. See if it has the qualities you want.

Sometimes it's the little things that make a difference. My husband bought a hammock that he set up in a shady spot on the terrace above our apartment. Each day, with a good book and a fresh cup of tea, he enjoyed an hour or two relaxing in his hammock in the breeze, setting down his book from time to time to admire the lush mountain views. If we decide to get a long-term place in Loja in the future, I know he will be looking for one with a good spot for his hammock.

There are also bigger issues you might never know of from simply looking at a picture. Does the neighborhood appeal to you? Does the house have a funny smell? Is there a mold problem? This is actually common in Loja, thanks to the frequent rains. Is the house in a part of town where the buildings tend to sink into the ground? Don't tie yourself down with a place you don't like or can't tolerate—come to Loja and house hunt in person!

If your Spanish skills are still in their earlier stages of development, you may want to hire a local person to assist you with your house-hunting process. Diana is an American expat living in Loja and has recently started the

"Loja Services Collective" to help with precisely these types of needs. She invites both foreigners and Ecuadorians to join in and provide services to expats and visitors to Loja. Visit **www.lojaservicescollective.blogspot.com** for more information.

If you're thinking of buying a house, I strongly encourage you to rent for a full year first to make sure that Loja is the right place for you. If it turns out not to be, you'll have a much easier time moving away if you don't have to sell a house!

Are you thinking of buying property and building a house in Ecuador? I recommend reading *Our House in the Clouds: Building a Second Life in the Andes of Ecuador*, by Judy Blankenship, to learn what the process is like from another expat couple who did it. To get it on Amazon go to **http://amzn.to/1Hr1UjX**

See the companion website for this book for more recommendations. **www.LilyAnnFouts.com/lojabonus**

Utilities and Other Bills

If you find an apartment that does not include utilities, internet, furniture, and other things of that nature, your next step will be to locate these resources and set them up in your new home.

Electricity

Your electric bill rate will depend on a variety of factors, including whether you have a dryer, whether you use a heater, the size of your home, and more. I've seen expats report their electric bills in Loja ranging from less than $15 to more than $30 per month.

The electric company is *Empresa Eléctrica Regional*

del Sur S.A. (ERSSA).

The main office is at *Olmedo* and *Rocafuerte*.

Other offices and places where you can pay your bill are listed on the website:

http://www.eerssa.com/puntos-de-pago/#
Phone number: 073700200.
Website: **www.eerssa.com**

Municipal Water

Water bills are also cheap. In 2014, expats reported bills around $8/month. More recently, the locals tell me, prices have gone up to help pay for all the work on the utilities in the city.

Municipo de Loja
Office: *Eguiguren* and *Bolívar*
Phone: 2570407

Garbage

You'll hear the garbage trucks before you see them. They drive through the streets playing a little whistling melody to let you know they're coming and remind you to get your trash out fast!

In Loja, garbage that can rot (basically compostable garbage) is separated from the rest of the garbage into two different cans—green and black. The garbage canisters are fairly small, but in our neighborhood each type of trash was picked up every other day, with the garbage trucks coming by a total of six days per week, so the trash doesn't build up much. Do keep the compost lid on to keep dogs out!

Garbage service is included in the water bill, and you must use their cans.

For a schedule of when to expect garbage service in

your neighborhood, check this site: **https://www.loja.gob.ec/contenido/horarios-de-recoleccion-de-basura**

Gas

Most stoves in Ecuador are gas. There is a program underway to switch all new stoves and water heaters to electric. Gas is heavily subsidized by the government and there is a plan to phase this out, but as of this writing that has not yet happened. It will likely take some time to implement and you may have a gas stove, at least at first. At our first apartment (in 2014) we had to buy our own gas. A cylinder of about 20 lbs cost under $2 and would last about 3 weeks for cooking and hot showers for 2 people. Gas is still incredibly cheap.

If you're lucky, you will have a water heater—either a tank or an on-demand system (called a *calefón*). The more common way to obtain hot water showers in Ecuador seems to be with the electric hot water shower heads, which have been dubbed "suicide showers" by some (don't touch the shower head once the water is on). My electrician husband is not a fan of them and has seen some truly atrocious wiring jobs in Latin America.

Within a short time of your arrival, you will probably see and hear the tuneful trucks driving around town, carrying cylinders of gas and five-gallon bottles of drinking water as they play the same notes over and over through a loudspeaker, much like an ice cream truck in the United States. If you need gas, you can listen out for these trucks and flag one down when it comes down your street. Most of the gas trucks are independent. You can also contact Loja Gas for delivery. Their information is on their website at **www.lojagas.com**.

I would recommend having two cylinders on hand so that when one runs out, you can switch the tanks and have plenty of time to get the first one refilled before the second one runs out.

Drinking Water

While some locals claim that the water in Loja is safe to drink from the faucet, others caution against it—especially for foreigners. One local told me that some parts of the city are safer than others, depending on which source the water came from. The city is currently working on their water facilities to ensure clean water for everyone, but in the meantime, to be on the safe side, we decided to avoid drinking from the tap.

There are several options for obtaining drinking water. The most expensive option is to buy bottled water in the smaller containers as needed from the store.

Another option is to buy it in the five-gallon containers from the melodious trucks selling gas. When you hear one coming, flag it down. You can purchase a dispenser for these large water jugs at any of many places around town, and set it up on your counter top.

We decided to buy a water purifier with a multi-stage filter for ourselves. Supermaxi and Gran AKI sell these filters, which when set up look a lot like a five gallon jug on a dispenser. The multi-stage filter is supposed to remove unsafe metals and bacteria, rendering tap water safe to drink. Simply set it up and pour water into the top portion. It will drip through the filter into a clean reservoir below, ready to drink.

In order to save both money and the environment, we filled reusable bottles with our filter and took them with us whenever we went out for a few hours. For extended trips away from home, we have a Steri-Pen, which is an ultraviolet wand that kills bacteria in under a minute. Simply stir up to a liter of tap water with the activated Steri-Pen for 90 seconds, and then the water should be safe to drink. You can find a Steri-Pen on Amazon at this URL: **http://amzn.to/1Helim1**

Phone
Like many people in the U.S. and elsewhere in the world, many people no longer have a land line and simply use their cell phone for everything. If you wish to follow suit, there are two main cellular providers available: Movistar and Claro. Less common cell phone providers includ CNT and Tuenti. Claro is the most popular cell phone provider in Ecuador. You will see vendors for Claro and Movistar all over town. Buy minutes to top up your phone as needed, or if you set up an Ecuadorian bank account you can also sign up for a cell phone plan.

For current details on plans and the cost of cell phone minutes, you can visit the providers' websites:
Claro: **www.claro.com.ec/portal/ec/sc/personas**
Movistar: **www.movistar.com.ec**
CNT: **www.cnt.gob.ec**
Tuenti: **www.tuenti.ec**
Cell phones, like all electronics, cost more in Ecuador than in the US. Some people prefer to buy a high quality phone (an *unlocked* GSM phone or it won't work!) and bring it to Ecuador with them. (If you would like to shop for one go to **http://amzn.to/1Kdyuba** to see what's on Amazon.)

The first time we went to Loja, we just purchased the cheapest "dumb phone" we could find there since expensive smart phones are a popular target of petty theft

—the most popular type of crime in Ecuador. We bought our phone and service from Claro.

On our second trip to Loja, we took an older unlocked iPhone and bought a SIM card from Movistar. The phone service was great, but I could not get the internet data to work, despite several attempts and visits to vendors and customer service centers.

Cell phone minutes and plans can also be more costly in Ecuador, so if you have a smart phone there I would recommend downloading an app such as Skype and making calls—especially international calls—via the app from a place with Wifi access.

If you want landline service (or the less popular government cell phone service), CNT services the Loja area. Their website is **www.cnt.gob.ec**.

Internet

The internet speed and quality in Loja is generally decent. During our visit in 2014, we shared high-speed service with our neighbors and rarely had problems watching videos or using Skype.

During our second visit to Loja, however, we stayed in a neighborhood affected by the utility work underway in the city. Internet was often no better than dial-up speed and the connection often dropped altogether. We called out a technician and toward the end of our six-week stay, and the service finally improved a little. In order to get my work done, I had to take my computer to a friend's house where the internet service was much better.

Many neighborhoods in Loja have internet cafes, so if you are not a heavy user of the internet, these services may be all you need—simply paying a small fee for the time you use. Also, the two city libraries, many of the cafes, and Mall Don Daniel also provide Wifi. Wifi signals are often available in the public squares, too, but I would caution against flashing expensive electronics out in the open.

For internet at home, the cost will vary depending on the speed you select. Obviously, the faster your connection the more you will pay. Many Ecuadorians pay $20 per month for their internet, but expats often pay $40 or more for higher speeds to stream movies, use Vonage phones, and so on. It is especially worth the investment for higher speeds if you work via the internet and require more bandwidth, as I do.

If your home does not include internet, here are the options:
- CNT, the same company that provides landline phone service: **www.cnt.gob.ec**
- TV Cable: **www.grupotvcable.com**

Cable TV

Companies you can choose from include CNT (**www.cnt.gob.ec**), Grupo TVCable (**www.grupotvcable.com**), and Direct TV (**www.directv.com.ec**). During our stay in 2017, we had cable TV in our apartment, provided by CNT—the same company who provided our internet and the landline phone. Oddly, despite the poor internet service, the TV and phone worked fine.

You can set up automatic bill pay for all your bills through an Ecuadorian bank, or via "Electric Cash" set up on your smart phone. **https://efectivo.ec**

Bank

Once you have your legal residency in Ecuador you may want to set up an Ecuadorian bank account. So which bank should you use? American expat James White recommends *Banco Pichincha*.
www.pichincha.com/portal/Inicio

He says, "I have a savings account and have everything (TV, Internet, mobile service) all on direct autopay. They are full service and have been easy to work with. They don't charge me to cash/deposit checks on my US accounts. However they don't deposit the money until they get it."

Furniture & Appliances

If you are planning to settle in Loja long-term and your home doesn't come furnished, you need to decide what you need and whether you want used or new furniture and appliances.

Appliances made outside Ecuador cost much more, but Ecuadorian-made appliances may not be to the same quality standard. The new fridge in our 2014 apartment quit working one time. We called the landlords and, true to form, it was a couple of days before anyone could come out and fix it. The good news is that there are plenty of repairmen accustomed to fixing broken appliances!

For new furniture, there are several places to choose from. I've heard the furniture stores in town mostly have similar prices, but you may still want to shop around and see if you can get better deals on last year's models versus the new models, etc. Price will also vary tremendously according to the quality. There are furniture markets where you can buy things at rock bottom prices, but as one expat said, it may give you splinters! You can also buy top-of-the-line stuff and spend as much or far more than you would in the U.S.

A few furniture stores that I have seen mentioned in the expat community are:
- Several furniture shops on *18 de Noviembre* - at least some of them do free deliveries.
- *Colineal* — large selection, but higher prices.
- *Casa de Muebles* — they have a reputation for being helpful.
- *Necusi* — on Riofrio, across from La Ganga; one expat ordered a custom sofa to the size and color she wanted
- *Arte Practik* — near *Necusi*—good selection.
- On Lourdes and Sucre — two shops selling office and household items
- Several expats have hired carpenters to make custom furniture for them.
- *Todo Hogar* and *Boyaca* — pricier, but good for things you can't find anywhere else.
- *Romar* and *Zerimar* — small stuff and plastics.
- *Hogar y Más* on *18 de Noviembre* in between *Colón* and *José Antonio Eguiguren* for appliances.
- *Almacenes Rosas Iñiguez* on *Mercadillo* in between *Bernardo Valdivieso* and *Olmedo* for furniture—some say this one is pricey.

If you are the frugal type like me who likes to find a good bargain on used furniture, a good place to start your search is OLX, which is like Craigslist. **http://ciudadloja.olx.com.ec**. However, it is my understanding that finding good used furniture in Ecuador is much harder than doing so in the U.S. If you have a way to transport the furniture, you may find it worthwhile to check with the expat communities in Vilcabamba and Cuenca, such as the Facebook groups and

GringoPost.com, to see if anyone is moving back to their home country and needs to get rid of some furniture quickly. Good luck!

Car or No Car?

One question you may be asking yourself is, should you get a car? Obviously there are pros and cons of vehicle ownership. Loja's driving scene may be more exciting than what you are used to at home, but there is actually some order in its chaos—much more so than many other Latin American cities I have visited. I think I could learn to be comfortable driving in Loja's traffic. Surprisingly, I haven't seen many accidents anywhere in Ecuador, though we did see some small dings in many vehicles. If hectic driving doesn't bother you, the next question to ask is whether the expense is worth the convenience.

If you have a family or a large dog that you like to take places, then having a car may make good sense. Our neighbors from Spain decided to get one when they found that traveling with their Yellow Labrador (big dog) on public transportation was not feasible. When they then found out that they were expecting a baby, that sealed their decision and they had a car shortly after that. Another expat friend, Diana, found that when she had a regular job in Loja, having her own transportation saved her a lot of time, and she really likes the convenience.

Gas in Ecuador is subsidized by the government and far cheaper than I have seen it anywhere else in the world at around $1.50 per gallon, so you'll save money there. However, vehicles cost a lot more to buy, thanks to the import taxes. You won't be able to import your vehicle from the U.S. Also, the government subsidy on gas will not be around forever, so bear that in mind.

I've heard mixed stories on insurance costs. The basic coverage required by law, called *SOAT*, is actually cheap. However, there are conflicting stories as to what is actually compensated with a comprehensive insurance plan (which is not required by law)—and what such a plan would cost. I have also heard that the body shops are relatively inexpensive if you wind up in a fender bender, so some people simply pay for those incidents out of pocket. See more details about driving and vehicle ownership on the companion website at **www.LilyAnnFouts.com/lojabonus**.

The other thing you will want is a secure place to park your car at night. Most homes and apartment buildings have a gated area that you can pull a vehicle into. Keep this in mind while you are house hunting if you anticipate buying a car.

It is tough to say for certain, but I believe I would prefer to avoid the expense and responsibility of vehicle ownership and choose to live in an area with easy access to the public transportation, which is so frequent and goes to so many places that it makes it easy to live without a car. Other expats feel differently and don't know how they ever managed without buying their cars. They are certainly much faster and more convenient than public transportation, and could be essential if you have a job requiring a commute or just have less free time and flexibility.

On occasions when we needed to travel beyond the realm of the public transportation system, we hired a driver (for example, to go to the trailhead inside Podocarpus National Park—see Chapter Nine).

A couple of drivers in Loja whom I've seen

recommended by expats include:
- **Roberto at 0988752654.** He speaks English. James White, an expat in Loja, says "He has a clean cab (near new) and is a very safe driver. He is prompt and professional." I have seen him recommended by others as well.
- **Lucas at 0980538272.** A "wonderful English-speaking taxi driver."

Diana Jesuroga, the administrator of the *Loja, Ecuador for English Speakers* Facebook group also offers services not only driving but also translating and assisting with other needs through her organization, the *Loja Services Collective.* She can be reached via e-mail at AllAboutLoja@gmail.com. For more information, see **lojaservicescollective.blogspot.com**.

Most taxi companies do not operate after midnight. If you have an early morning bus to catch out of town, as we once did, one taxi company offering 24-hour service is called *Andina Sur*, at *2107570*. This company was recommended to us by a local and they were great. Also, do not forget about the new taxi app, Ktaxi, which is a great way to call a taxi right to your door via your smartphone.

For more information, visit the companion website: **www.LilyAnnFouts.com/lojabonus**.

And this leads me to the next topic: making friends. In the next chapter, I'll tell you some stories about how we made new friends in Loja, and offer some ideas and suggestions for how you might start meeting the locals.

CHAPTER TWELVE
Making Friends

    Thankfully, making friends in Loja is not a terribly hard thing to do, since the people there are naturally friendly and will probably be curious about you.
    The best way to make friends, in my opinion, is to first look for activities that you are interested in. Yoga, cooking, hiking, music, crafts, dancing, art, cycling, writing, running, civic clubs, churches or religious organizations, and so on. Find groups of people doing those things that interest you and you'll naturally have something in common to bond over. Search for Facebook

groups, check out advertisements on bulletin boards, and ask around. Access the companion website at **www.LilyAnnFouts.com/lojabonus** for some links to start with.

I'm a fairly shy person, so I was a little nervous about how I would make friends when we first moved to Loja. It did take a little time at first, but once we went out and started interacting with people, things began to happen naturally.

One of the first things we did was try to befriend the people right in our apartment building. We invited our Spanish neighbors on the floor below ours to come to our place for dinner one evening. Later on, they invited us to their place. As more people moved into the apartment building, these gradually turned into community potluck events every few weeks.

We also walked around town a lot and opened ourselves to interaction with people. One day, we were out exploring the hills on the southern edge of the city. As we walked through the last *barrio* before reaching the wilderness—*Punzara Grande*—Mélida, the friendly woman I described in Chapter Nine, engaged us in conversation. When she learned that we enjoyed hiking, she pointed out several trails in the area for us to explore, and then invited us to return to her neighborhood on Sunday at 2 p.m. for *bailoterapia*—a dance fitness workout known as Zumba in the U.S. In Ecuador *bailoterapia* is sponsored by the government, which pays instructors to teach the fitness classes in neighborhoods throughout the country, free to the public. (Although we have discovered that when the government contract is up, sometimes instructors will continue to teach the class if each participant pays a small amount, until they can get their contract renewed.)

The next Sunday we returned to the neighborhood. The instructor drove up, set up some large speakers on the volleyball court (common in every neighborhood), cranked up music so loud that any north American neighborhood would be calling the cops, and led the community in a vigorous workout. By the end of the hour we dripped with sweat, but wow! It was like a party!

After we returned home I realized I had left my sunglasses back in *Punzara Grande*. Frustrated with myself and knowing I would likely never see them again, I bought a new pair the next time we went downtown. The following Sunday we returned to the neighborhood for more *bailoterapia*. Mélida came up to me, holding out my sunglasses for me. "You dropped these last time you were here," she said. I was impressed, figuring that if I left something laying around it would disappear, which is what often happens in Latin America. In Loja we experienced many instances of honesty, fairness and generosity.

When I told our Spanish neighbors about the *bailoterapia* sessions, they told us that they had seen something similar in our own neighborhood in the morning while out walking their dog.

The next morning we left our apartment a little before 7:00 to investigate, and sure enough. Every weekday morning–and sometimes on Saturday, too–there were two one-hour *bailoterapia* sessions, each attracting 100 or more people! The dancers filled the street, blocking it off from 6:00 to 8:00 every morning.

We heard the music from several blocks away–not quite all the way to our apartment, but almost! We attended almost every morning. Great workout, and wonderful way to interact with the community! To read a blog post and see photos and a video about *bailoterapia*, visit the companion web page. (Access at **www.LilyAnnFouts.com/lojabonus**.)

Through our involvement with the *bailoterapia* classes, we made several new friends in our neighborhood, later sharing meals, walks, and great conversations together. When I told them I was interested in learning to cook some food from the area, they came over to our house and helped me cook a traditional breakfast one morning after our workout!

Every couple of days I checked the Loja event page on Facebook. One day I saw an advertisement for yoga classes, a skill I had been wanting to improve. Keith and I signed up and began attending the classes. During the first class, as everyone was going around and introducing themselves and saying why they were there and what they hoped to gain from the yoga class, I shared honestly that we were interested in yoga, but that we also were interested in getting to know people on a social level as we were new in town. This drew friendly smiles from our classmates, and we had several good interactions with our instructor and fellow students there. After class one day Keith offered to teach some swing dancing before the next yoga class, which was great fun.

Toward the end of our time in Loja, we also found a large, active hiking group called LojAventura and joined them for an amazing excursion to Yacuri National Park, which I will describe in further detail in Chapter Sixteen. During that trip we formed several more new friendships. If you enjoy hiking and adventurous excursions, visit their Facebook page at **www.facebook.com/lojaventura**.

Of course we were not in Loja long enough for any of the friendships to become particularly close, but we kept in touch with many of our friends after we returned to the U.S. During our second trip, we were able to deepen some of these relationships. I trust that the friendships will continue to grow as we return to Loja and get to know our friends better each time. I genuinely miss these people and look forward to seeing them again. We enjoyed meaningful conversations over shared experiences that we all were interested in.

Other expats I know in Loja have developed good friendships with their landlords, who invite them to participate in family celebrations and help them learn about the ways of life in Loja. Through their landlords they have gotten to know other people in town, too.

Hopefully this inspires you to seek out activities you enjoy and begin interacting with other people there.

Here are a few random ideas for making friends:
- Go to the parks and interact with people there. You'll find people of all ages socializing and having a great time there, especially on the weekends. Exercise in the park in the mornings!
- Get to know the neighbors in your apartment building or on your street. Take some food or small gifts to them or invite them to join you for a cup of coffee or a meal.
- Join a *bailoterapia* group in your neighborhood for a great workout and get to know the people there.
- Find a volleyball game in progress (this is a popular sport in every neighborhood) and visit with the people gathered there.
- Find someone to teach you a new instrument or help you improve on an instrument you already play (Loja is full of musicians—check OLX at

http://loja.olx.com.ec/clases-cursos-cat-876) If we set up a more permanent base in Loja I may try to find a cello and an instructor!
- If you already play an instrument, ask around to see if there are any jam sessions you can join or if anyone would be interested in starting one.
- Find someone who loves to cook who would be willing to teach you how to make the traditional foods of Loja and Ecuador.
- If someone invites you to come to their home for coffee or a meal, accept the invitation! (Unless your gut tells you the person is untrustworthy, but that is unlikely.) Invite them to your home as well.
- If you have a family, take your kids to places and events where they can make friends and get to know their friends' parents.

I've heard several Ecuadorians comment that they feel foreigners are closed and unfriendly. "We try to extend friendship, but they have a very closed community," they say. I realize the expats may not be unfriendly on purpose, but I know what the Ecuadorians are talking about. Having lived in Mexico for five years, I realized that Latino cultures are much closer to the people around them. Everybody knows everybody else, and people drop by to visit all the time. Neighbors are almost like extended family. In that culture, people welcome each other into their homes and are much less reserved. When we came back to live in the U.S. after five years in Mexico, American people seemed distant and reserved to me. In the U.S., many of us don't even know our neighbors. That was hard for me after life in Mexico.

Let's learn to open up to our Ecuadorian neighbors and

friends. Ask them questions about themselves and their families and their lives. Answer the questions that they ask you. Accept their invitations and invite them in return. Bring back the old art of hospitality. Respect their ways of life. Share your life with them. You'll get what you put into it and more. Warm up a little, and trust me—you'll be amazed at the friendships you form.

CHAPTER THIRTEEN
Culture Clashes

　　Inevitably, as you interact with people you will run into frustrations and misunderstandings, especially when you're trying to accomplish something and you want it to happen quickly and efficiently. It's all part of the adventure of adopting a new culture. Our apartment story in Chapter Eleven is a perfect illustration of this! If you've been skipping around in this book, flip back and read that story before proceeding in this chapter, because it will provide some context for the cultural differences I'll be explaining here.
　　Unless you have spent a significant amount of time interacting with someone from another culture, you may

be quite unaware of some of your own cultural values. Things you've always taken for granted will suddenly become points of friction with people who have always taken a conflicting point of view for granted. Below are just some ways in which you will likely encounter cultural differences.

Communication Styles

As someone from North America, Europe or Australia, you may value openness, honesty, and directness. "Say what you mean and mean what you say," right? Not so in Latin America. Typically, if they think something could be upsetting or offensive to you, they will not come out and say it. Remember our apartment story? Cristian never said no to us. If we asked for something, he would say "Yes, of course," but in Latin America that might mean "maybe" or it might mean "no." Above all, it means that they don't want to say anything unpleasant. Instead, they will say what they think you want to hear, then find a way to let you know the real situation passively and indirectly.

An extremely common way for Latin Americans to avoid saying no directly is to say *"mañana"* (tomorrow). While I was living in Mexico I learned that when someone came to our door to sell us something, if I just said *"mañana"* that pretty much meant I wasn't interested—not that I actually wanted them to come back the next day. Our Ecuadorian landlords also said *"mañana"* a lot, as you may recall from my story. In contexts like that, *mañana* simply means "maybe someday."

Another difference in communication styles comes in the way we speak, and I'm not just talking about English vs. Spanish. While in North America we may value being succinct and to the point in our speech, Latin Americans are much more "flowery" and descriptive. When you ask a question, you may expect a quick one or two word reply and get a whole story—or at least a much more elaborate statement, setting up some context—instead.

While at the market with an Ecuadorian friend, for example, you may innocently point to an unusual fruit you have never seen before and ask, "What is that?" and expect them to simply give you the name of the fruit. Instead they may reply with, "This is what is known as a *granadilla*. It is sweet like a mango, but juicy and it has crunchy little seeds inside. It is eaten fresh, or in juices or smoothies. You open it up like this…" and they will mime the process of eating the fruit.

Also, observe the speeches at events such as the weekly *Jueves Culturales* program. Where in the United States an announcer might give a brief synopsis of the next performer's accomplishments and end with, "Please help me welcome Juan Cantante," the Ecuadorian announcers become very flowery.

"Ladies and gentlemen, esteemed guests who are joining us here this beautiful evening, it is my great pleasure and honor to present to you today, a distinguished singer. A singer who has traveled across the world, to many countries, to perform for the wonderful people of those faraway lands. Now this performer is giving us a great privilege, and doing us the great honor, of coming here to Loja today, to perform for us…." The elaborateness of the speech will vary from person to person, but overall Latin Americans are much more verbose.

This tendency to speak a lot before getting to the point is important to note. Latin Americans are social creatures and like to talk about family and fun things before getting down to business. The pace of life is much more relaxed, and if you can learn to hold back on your impulse to get "straight to business" then you may find that you'll have much smoother interactions and often even receive much better deals on rental agreements, major purchases, and every day business interactions. For example, if you go to a corner store to pick up some cooking oil, greet the lady behind the counter and ask her how she is doing before simply saying, "Do you have cooking oil?" It is hard to break the habit of getting straight to the point, but doing so comes across as cold and abrupt to a Latin American. Your business transactions and personal relationships will go much better in Latin America if you learn to slow down and treat each person as a complete human being.

A final point to consider for communication differences is the volume of our speech. As Americans we tend to speak much louder than Ecuadorians. I personally can get pretty loud when I am excited. Observe Ecuadorians in conversation with one another on a bus, in a restaurant, or in a business setting. Observe American tourists and expats in similar settings. Notice the difference in the volume of their speech! Ecuadorians will find you much more enjoyable to be around if you can lower your voice when you speak.

Concepts of Time

Your concept of time will also likely be different than a Latin American's concept of time. This is a source of great frustration for many expats, who view time in a linear fashion, in fairly rigid terms of deadlines and schedules. Latin Americans, in contrast, view time as a relative and flexible thing that can be shifted around as needed to accommodate more important things, such as family and friends.

While there is a movement underway to be more punctual, and some people tend to be more punctual than others, in general Latin Americans do not place a high value on punctuality. Schedules and deadlines are rarely set in stone when it comes to informal events, though they are sometimes adhered to more in some formal business and government settings. For example, we noticed that classes and intercity buses typically operated on schedule, but parties, concerts and other social events sometimes started over an hour beyond their scheduled times. Take this as your cue and show up late if you're invited to someone's home for an informal occasion. They will expect this, and may even feel awkward if you show up on time. Being late to events is so commonplace in Latin America that nobody even apologizes for it. It is just the way things are.

Construction projects are also frequently delayed beyond their deadlines, as you remember from our experience trying to get a stove installed in our apartment during our first stint in Loja. The second time we went to Loja, we had internet problems, due in part to a damage in the network caused by construction going on in the city. Large sections of the city have been disrupted thanks to this project, and construction is likely to continue beyond the deadline. It took weeks for the internet company to come to our apartment and investigate. This may exasperate you, but take a deep breath and try not to take it too personally. This is how things operate in Latin America, and it requires a lot of patience and understanding. Being confrontational and pushy will only make things worse.

Concepts of Individuality

The American Way is all about individuality. As individuals we control our destiny, we challenge authority, we think for ourselves, we value our independence and we seek personal fulfillment. Not so much in Latin America, where a more collectivist mindset exists. In Latin America people look out for each other and strive for group harmony, following time-honored traditions and customs.

This is especially evident in the way Latin Americans view family. The extended family—aunts, uncles, grandparents, cousins—are as close to each other as the nuclear family is in North America. They even adopt friends and neighbors into this close-knit group, and we were honored to be treated like family by some of our close friends and neighbors in Mexico. Whereas in North America we may push our children to become independent and move out on their own, Latin American children sometimes continue to live at home into adulthood. Typically they also care for their elderly parents, instead of sending them to assisted living or nursing home facilities.

They also view and treat authority figures with much more respect. The Spanish language is even structured to speak formally to older people, formal business acquaintances and authority figures, and informally to friends or people who are considered to have less authority than you—such as children or subordinates.

You can imagine how a foreigner coming into this culture might cause offense without even meaning to. Speaking disparagingly of someone they view as an authority figure, family member or close friend could hurt your friendship.

Concepts of Personal Space

In North America we tend to keep everyone but our close family members at arm's length—literally. If someone we don't know well stands much closer than an arm's length away while talking to us, we tend to squirm in discomfort and feel an almost irresistible impulse to take a step backwards. However, standing closer than arm's length is common in Ecuador, and if you continually step back from them you may be seen as a cold and distant person. You'll need to get used to being very close to people in Ecuador, especially in public areas such as on public transportation and in markets.

Once you get to know someone in Ecuador, greetings also become more intimate. Rather than a handshake, women greet other women and men with a kiss on the right cheek. Men greet each other with a handshake or sometimes a loose hug with a pat on the shoulder.

These concepts of personal space apply also to privacy. Remember the story about the curtains in our apartment? Life in Ecuador may be less private than what you are used to. This extends beyond physical privacy and can include questions about yourself that you may view as "personal." Chances are, your new Ecuadorian friends are not just being nosy. They are trying to get to know you, and by being open with them you may more easily earn their trust and friendship. If you take offense at their questions you might be seen as a rude person.

Formality

Latin Americans tend to be more formal than we are. Whereas we could show up to church or a symphony in jeans and T-shirts in our country, Ecuadorians tend to dress nicely for such occasions. Even in the obviously poorer neighborhoods, people keep themselves clean, neat and tidy. Showing up to the store in uncombed hair and pajama bottoms (as often happens in our Walmart stores in the U.S.) would be unthinkable in Ecuador. In some situations I actually felt quite under-dressed compared to the Ecuadorians around me. On our second trip to Loja, we made sure to take a nicer change of clothes and shoes for more formal occasions (the symphony, etc.).

In addition to their appearance, Ecuadorians are also quite formal with their business transactions. There is lots of paperwork for everything. Many museums, the national parks, and other sites of interest often require visitors to sign in with their passport or national ID number. From stories I have heard of people going through the process of becoming legal residents, all paperwork must be "just so." Bureaucracy is alive and well in Ecuador.

Gender Roles

Men and women relate to each other differently than what we are used to in the US. There is still a certain level of inequality between men and women in most of the world—and in some regions this is more blatant. Latin America has a reputation for machismo. Single women especially need to be careful in Latin America, since a woman without a man is almost viewed as "prey" for the men to hunt. If you are not interested in more than friendship, be careful to do nothing that would lead them to think otherwise. Single women may also find it a little more challenging to make female friends because they might be viewed as competition for the men.

While we were living in Mexico, this is something my single mom had to deal with on a regular basis. She worked hard to establish and maintain her reputation as an "honorable woman" by insisting that men coming to see her for medical purposes be accompanied by their wives at all times. When people realized that she had no designs on the men there, she was able to develop good friendships with both men and women.

In the U.S. we think nothing of inviting a friend of the opposite sex into our homes to visit, but such an invitation in Latin America when nobody else is around could well be interpreted by the person you're inviting as wanting to be more than friends. Observers might even think that there is an intimate physical relationship happening behind closed doors. Exercise caution! When male friends came over to visit my mom in Mexico, she kept the door open so passers-by could see that nothing was going on.

Comfort and Convenience

In our first-world countries, we are used to comfort and convenience. Hot running water. Functioning appliances. Reliable and comfortable transportation. Climate-controlled rooms. Dependable electricity. Satisfaction guarantees and refunds. Well-stocked grocery stores that always have what we need.

In Latin America, you can't take any of these things for granted. Things are improving every year, but Ecuador is still a developing country. Every day, be prepared for an adventure. At some point, the water will quit running. The power will randomly go out. The internet won't work right. You'll run out of hot water in the middle of a shower. The bus you're riding will break down or be so overcrowded that your feet will go numb as you stand in the aisle. The flight you're on will get diverted and you won't get a refund. You won't be able to find the key ingredient to make your favorite dish. Every single one of these things has happened to us or someone we know in Ecuador.

Ecuadorians and other Latin Americans take it all in stride. They know how to relax and be happy in spite of the difficulties. Rarely do you see people getting angry about these things. Just sit back and take a deep breath, wait it out, or find another way around the problem. Things will work out, or you'll learn to live with it. Don't get angry and yell at the locals about it. You'll discover it's only counter-productive to do so.

If you can learn to respect and live with the cultural differences you'll find in Loja, you will find yourself much more accepted, and much more able to develop true and meaningful friendships there, which is a rewarding experience. Still, you will probably experience periods of homesickness and a desire to mingle with people who understand your own culture, and for that, you may want to make some friends in the expat community. There are a few expats in town, but from Loja, the closest major concentration of foreigners is in Vilcabamba. We'll explore that town in the next chapter.

CHAPTER FOURTEEN
Vilcabamba

Crime has become more of a problem in Vilcabamba in recent years. Overall, Ecuador is a safe country, and Vilcabamba is generally safe, too–but people who come in from other countries and flash their wealth tend to become targets for muggings. Our friends in Loja urged us to be careful when they heard we were going to Vilcabamba.

We also saw more beggars in Vilcabamba than Loja—and Vilcabamba is only a tiny fraction of the size of Loja. Many foreigners, thinking they are doing something good, give money to beggars, which encourages more people to beg and can create dependency. Ecuador seems to have a good system in place to take care of its people, and our friends in Loja confirmed that there is no good reason for people to beg. I can't recall seeing any homeless people at all anywhere in Ecuador, and beggars are rare—less common than in U.S. cities in most places. Hunger is practically non-existent due to the wonderful climate and resulting abundance of food in the country.

The "gringo economy" is in full force in Vilcabamba. Most restaurants, hotels, and groceries cost more than they do in Loja. I see the locals sizing up the foreigners and quoting them higher prices in Vilcabamba, whereas in Loja we were almost always treated fairly and given the same price as everyone else, with few exceptions. Many expats in Vilcabamba own businesses, and often charge much higher prices for things than locals would. Expats are buying up the property in the area and reselling it at prices that many locals can no longer afford.

I so badly wanted to adore Vilcabamba. I'd heard a lot of wonderful things about the town, and before arriving I thought it might be a place I would like to live someday. It is truly a beautiful place. The weather is basically perfect—warmer than Loja, but not suffocatingly hot. And even when it rains for several hours on end—as it did at various times during our multi-day visit over Carnaval weekend—it never felt cold to me. The area is so beautiful and pristine, and some great people live there—expats and locals alike.

As I've mentioned earlier in this book, I wouldn't personally want to live in Vilcabamba because I feel that the expat-to-local ratio in the population is beyond the tipping point and I saw a growing chasm of resentment and distrust between the two groups, which made me sad.

To be honest, it ruined the magic of Vilcabamba for me, because one of my greatest joys is to see cultures coming together and building bridges of friendship with one another—not drifting apart and becoming fearful and resentful of each other. There are definitely some good friendships between locals and expats in Vilcabamba, but I see the trend progressing in the wrong direction. I felt a real difference in the way the locals acted toward me in Vilcabamba compared to Loja.

There are plenty of people who would disagree with me, however. "One person's heaven is another person's hell," as they say. Obviously, many expats love Vilcabamba and wouldn't want to live anywhere else!

Despite my opinions of Vilcabamba as a place to live, I think it can be a great place to visit—for its weather, its scenery, and for the opportunity to develop some friendships with people from all over the world who call it home. For the homesick expat who just needs a break to speak in their mother tongue with someone who will have no trouble understanding their culture, Vilcabamba might provide that relief. It's also a great place for the foodie who can't find enough variety or satisfaction in the restaurants of Loja—especially if said foodie is a vegetarian.

Vilcabamba is a small little town, with a pretty town square in front of the cathedral and lots of quaint shops and restaurants of many kinds within a couple of blocks in any direction. Most of the expats live out in the country surrounding the town. Like Loja, Vilcabamba is a great place for the lover of the outdoors—hikers, birdwatchers, and photographers.

After spending time in Loja, you may be shocked to hear English widely spoken around you as you stroll through Vilcabamba. The prices of things may also come as a bit of a shock. If you're on a slim budget I suggest seeking out the restaurants frequented by the natives.

Lodging and Food

Hotels generally cost about 50% more than they do in Loja. However, if you don't mind hiking a bit, I recommend the river cabins at Rumi Wilco reserve (**rumiwilco.com**), managed by a family from Argentina. You will have to carry your food and luggage for about a ten minute walk down a trail, so pack light. The cabins are simple but well-appointed with everything you could need to stay comfortably, including bathrooms with hot showers, full kitchens with refrigerator, stove, blender, plenty of dishes and utensils, and a hammock! I felt like they were actually a pretty good bargain for the price, which is currently $36 per night for two people.

For the extremely budget-conscious, if you enjoy camping and have your camping gear, there is also a campground in the same area as the cabins, with access to a bathroom, shower, and full kitchen (including a fridge) for $5 per night per camper. The reserve has other reasonably priced lodging options as well. Visit their website for full details and current rates.

We have not stayed there ourselves yet, but have heard from several people that Izhcayluma is another nice place to stay, and it does look delightful. **www.izhcayluma.com**

There are numerous hostales and Airbnb options throughout town.

One of Vilcabamba's strong points and a major draw for me was the wide variety of foods—especially ethnic and vegetarian options—that are difficult to find in many other parts of Ecuador.

Wander around town and see what culinary surprises you discover! One time we found a street vendor selling a great meal—curried rice and a big salad—for only $1 per "plate" (actually it was served on a banana leaf), so you never know what you'll find.

For fresh, delicious Mexican food, try a restaurant called "El Colibrí." They serve generous portions and prices seemed reasonable. Another popular Mexican spot is "Agave Blu" in the central plaza.

A newer restaurant which we enjoyed on our most recent trip, and which has quickly risen in popularity, is "Murano," which serves an eclectic mix of dishes from Mediterranean to Italian to Spanish.

Activities

If you don't like to walk or try new restaurants, there is not a whole lot else to do in Vilcabamba, unless you happen to visit during a festival like we did. If you enjoy hiking in the great outdoors, though, rejoice!

For a shorter walk, pay a small fee and stroll through the small zoo, filled mostly with aviaries. Next to the zoo there is also a swimming pool with water slides.

Rumi Wilco Reserve, mentioned above for its lodging options, is also a great hiking spot with a whole system of trails—some level, along the river valley—and others steep, up the mountain from which you'll have great views of the whole valley. There's a donation box at the entrance, and they use the funds to help maintain and preserve the park. Deposit your donation, pick up a trail map and set out to explore as much or as little as you feel like! There are lots of beautiful birds to see, so if you're a birder be sure to bring your binoculars.

Podocarpus National Park also has an entrance outside Vilcabamba, with a trail leading far into the mountains. We hiked several miles of this at one point but had to turn around in order to catch our bus back to Loja before dark.

Vilcabamba vs. Loja as a Place to Live
Table 11.1

	Vilcabamba	**Loja**
Size	Estimates vary wildly, most say around 5,000.	Pop. 180,617 city/214,855 metro
Weather	Close to perfect. Warmer and sunnier than Loja, but not sweltering. I don't think it ever gets truly cold.	Avg. 73°F high/45°F low, 35 inches/yr of precipitation, 136 rainy days per year and 1,736 sunshine hours per year. 75% avg. humidity.
Medical Facilities	A small basic clinic	Several clinics and hospitals
Airport	None	Small, about 45 min. out
Shopping	Few options. No major stores, just smaller *tiendas* and a weekly outdoor market. Bigger needs require trip to Loja.	All the basics covered. Supermaxi & Gran AKI stores, several markets, furniture stores, health food store.
Housing	Easier to find expat-friendly housing. Probably	Difficult to find anything furnished. Unfurnished can be

	easier to find used furniture from expats moving out.	cheap but owners often want 6-12 month lease. Furniture hard to find used.
English Speakers	All over the place.	Few and far between.
Immersion Into Ecuadorian Culture	Easy to get sucked into the expat community if one is not careful.	Not only easy, but necessary to do since few expats live there.
Cultural Events	Not a whole lot. The big event each year is Carnaval.	Occasional festivals, Symphony orchestra & other music, Jueves Culturales every week..
Museums & Architectural Attractions	Not much.	A few. Everything is in Spanish.
Hiking	Rumi Wilco Refuge, Podocarpus NP, and various other trails.	Easy access to many trails from town, big city parks, Podocarpus NP a few kilometers away.
Other Activities	It seems the expat community usually has things going, often of the "New Age" type—yoga, meditation, etc.	Socialize with the locals, find people who could tutor you in music or Spanish for a fee or trade for English lessons.

Overall I think Vilcabamba is a great place to visit and enjoy a quiet change of pace and scenery from the city of Loja. However, if you find Loja to be too small and your "break" would be something bigger and more exciting, then jump on a bus and head the other direction—to the big, beautiful city of Cuenca! We'll explore that destination in the next chapter.

CHAPTER FIFTEEN
Cuenca

You've probably already heard a lot about Cuenca if you're looking at Ecuador as a potential place to live. It's one of the most popular expat destinations in the world right now, particularly among retirees. I'm not a Cuenca expert, having only spent a week there. I will leave more experienced authors to fill you in on all the various activities, lodging and food options available (and there are many), but I'll use this space to share my observations of how Cuenca compares to Loja as a place to live.

I'll be honest: Cuenca may be a better option for most

people. If you're starting with no prior experience in the language or culture, Cuenca could provide a much easier transition than Loja. This is especially true if you haven't moved much at all in your life and you don't like change. I suspect that if you've made it this far into the book, though, you might be a person who can handle change well. The fact that you're even considering a move abroad makes you more adventurous than the average person out there.

How does Cuenca compare to Loja?

Cuenca is a much bigger city than Loja. If you desire a more urban lifestyle, more cultural events, more architectural wonders and museums, more culinary options, easier access to an airport, more shopping options, and more English speakers, Cuenca is the better option. There's a much more developed infrastructure for the expat community, so finding a place to live and figuring out how everything works is much easier, especially if your Spanish is limited. If nothing else, Cuenca may be a great place to start when you first move to Ecuador, while you explore Loja and other regions for a possible future move.

Cuenca also makes more sense for those for whom good medical care may be an important factor. I have read of more than one person who has left Ecuador because of health issues. The consensus is that Cuenca has pretty good health care facilities, Loja has more limited facilities, and for very serious conditions it's possible you may need to leave Ecuador altogether.

If you're a lover of the outdoors, a hiking and birdwatching enthusiast, feel more comfortable in smaller communities, have a good grasp of Spanish or a strong motivation to learn and, most importantly, truly wish to immerse yourself into the Ecuadorian culture, Loja could be the winner. If you're in relatively good health and don't foresee needing high quality medical care on a regular basis, Loja shouldn't be a problem. The city is big enough to have all the main things you would need, but small enough not to feel like a major urban center. Within a few minutes of anywhere in town you can be enjoying nature on a trail outside the city, and if you feel a need for some cultural activities the symphony and *Jueves Culturales* provide regular free concerts.

Cuenca is a little higher in elevation than Loja and as a result can be colder than Loja. However, Loja has a few more cloudy days, slightly more annual rainfall, and generally cooler nights. Both cities enjoy a mostly steady temperature year-round as well as rainy seasons and dry seasons. Both usually see at least some sun every day, even in the rainy season. Loja can be quite misty in the morning, but it usually burns off by midday.

As for the sentiment toward expats, I did feel less welcome in Cuenca than I did in Loja. In the *mercado* we were charged a little more in Cuenca than we had been in Loja. The vendors seemed more argumentative and aloof. I had the distinct impression that they had experienced some negative encounters with other expats and/or tourists in the past. As we walked around, we could see that certain businesses were patronized almost exclusively by foreigners, and the locals kept more to themselves— elsewhere. However, this was in the touristed downtown area. One expat told me that in Cuenca it was almost expected by both the locals and the expats that she would want to socialize with the expats, which made it harder for her to form friendships with locals. It is possible that in some neighborhoods in other parts of the city there is less of a foreigner influence and it could be easier to integrate with the locals and develop some friendships.

In general I prefer smaller cities, which is why I am biased toward Loja. However, Cuenca's size does give it an advantage in that its sizable expat population does not affect it as much as it does a small town like Vilcabamba. For the expat who still wants to integrate with the local culture but prefers a larger city, Cuenca affords that option thanks to its sheer size. It is possible to walk away from the large concentration of expats and settle in a much more local neighborhood. Because of this, I would actually consider living in or near Cuenca myself.

I've put together a table that summarizes the features of each city. I hope you will find it helpful if you're trying to decide between Cuenca and Loja.

Cuenca vs. Loja
Table 12.1

	Cuenca	Loja
Size	Pop. 400,000 city/700,000 metro	Pop. 180,617 city/214,855 metro
Weather	Avg. 69°F high/49°F low, 28 inches/yr. of precipitation, 179 rainy days per year and 1,799 sunshine hours per year. 75% avg. humidity.	Avg. 73°F high/45°F low, 35 inches/yr of precipitation, 136 rainy days per year and 1,736 sunshine hours per year. 75% avg. humidity.
Medical Facilities	Better, more options	Fewer options, poorer reputation
Airport	Larger, right in	Small, about 45

	town	min. out
Shopping	Many options. Larger purchases such as building materials, furniture, etc much cheaper.	All the basics are covered. Supermaxi & Gran AKI, several markets, furniture stores, health food store.
Housing	Easier to find, especially furnished. More competition may help keep prices lower. Easier to find used furniture from expats moving out & new furniture is cheaper.	Difficult to find anything furnished. Unfurnished can be cheap but owners often want 6-12 month lease. Furniture more expensive to buy, hard to find used.
English Speakers	More common; thousands of expats.	Few—most are down in Vilcabamba
Immersion Into Ecuadorian Culture	Very possible to do, but could get sucked into the expat community if one is not careful.	Not only easy, but necessary to do since very few expats live there.
Cultural Events	Very frequent; symphony, dance performances, theater, & more; things happening all the time	Symphony orchestra & other bands & Jueves Culturales each week. Annual International Festival of Live Arts.
Museums & Architectural	Lots! UNESCO World Heritage city. Some things in	A few. Everything is in Spanish.

Attractions	English.	
Hiking	Nice city parks, El Cajas NP 30 km outside the city	Easy access to many trails from town, Podocarpus NP a few kilometers away, nice city parks.
Other Activities	Plenty to choose from inside and outside the expat community.	Socialize with the locals, find people who could tutor you in music or Spanish for a fee or trade for English lessons.

I think a good analogy for Loja and Cuenca would be a good sized U.S. town compared to a major U.S. city. Think Spokane vs. Seattle in Washington, Pueblo vs. Denver in Colorado, or Santa Fe vs. Albuquerque in New Mexico. The smaller cities have everything you would need, but the larger cities have a much more vibrant cultural scene, more shopping options, better medical facilities and a much larger population.

To learn more about Cuenca, I highly recommend the blog by Bryan and Dena Haines, *Inside Ecuador*. **gringosabroad.com/ecuador**

There are also many books and e-books written about Cuenca which you can find on Amazon.com. For recommendations, visit this book's companion website. (Access at **www.LilyAnnFouts.com/lojabonus**.)

In the next chapter, we'll explore some other towns within a few hours of Loja. Let's go!

CHAPTER SIXTEEN
Other Towns Near Loja

One of the great things about Ecuador—or many other parts of the world—is how easy it is to get around, even without a car. While we lived in Loja, several times we hopped on one of the many regular buses leaving town and went to explore some of the surrounding areas for a day or two. Most of these towns were within the Province of Loja.

Catamayo
The first town many encounter inside the province is

Catamayo, which is where the regional airport is. It was also our first introduction to the Province as we rode through on the bus from Guayaquil to Loja. Catamayo has a warm, dry climate compared to Loja and we noticed many sugar cane crops in the area. We went through Catamayo several times en route to and from other places. Bus tickets for the 45-minute ride between Catamayo and Loja cost $1.30. For some additional information and videos from Catamayo, visit the companion website. (Access at **www.LilyAnnFouts.com/lojabonus**.)

El Cisne

The biggest event in the Loja Province each year is the annual pilgrimage of *La Virgen de El Cisne.* Attracting hundreds of thousands of devout Catholics from all over the country and neighboring countries, this pilgrimage takes place each August and begins in the little town of El Cisne, way up in the mountains north of Catamayo (bus tickets for the 90-minute trip cost $2.50). For three days, the sea of pilgrims carries the Virgin on their shoulders from one town to another, ending 71 kilometers later in the city of Loja. El Cisne is the Virgin's home for most of the year. Her enormous powder-blue *santuario* dominates the tiny town.

The day Keith and I visited, it was pouring rain and we seemed to be the only tourists. The town is obviously accustomed to quite a stream of tourists, judging by all the souvenir shops lining the streets leading to the cathedral, but many of them were closed.

We sat in for the last few minutes of mass, unable to understand most of the words as they echoed about in the massive building. The echoes gave the music an ethereal quality.

The few tourist shop owners that were open that day seemed eager to make a sale or two. We brought smiles to their faces by buying several souvenirs to take back to our families. We also bought some hot cups of *morocho*—a drink made of milk and corn—from one of the street vendors to help stave off the moist chill we felt from the rain. El Cisne's elevation is higher than Loja's, so be sure to bring an extra layer in case the weather is cool. We walked around the cathedral and explored some more. Unfortunately we didn't see the museum, but several locals have since told me that it is very nice.

After a hot lunch at one of the local restaurants, we splashed our way back to the bus and returned to Loja.

For some pictures of El Cisne, visit the companion website. (Access at **www.LilyAnnFouts.com/lojabonus**.)

Malacatos

South of Loja, just a few minutes before you arrive in Vilcabamba, you pass through Malacatos. When we first passed through on the bus and I saw all the fancy homes with swimming pools, I thought there must be a lot of expats there. However, it turns out there are very few (though expat numbers are rising quickly). Most of the fancy homes are vacation homes owned by rich people from Loja. Many of the houses are fancy even by U.S. standards and have swimming pools in their yards. There are some wealthy people in Loja! Malacatos' climate is much warmer—similar to Vilcabamba's—and it's a great place to escape to when you tire of Loja's cooler days.

After several days of mostly cooler/wetter weather in Loja, I felt like getting out of town and heading for some warmth and sun. Malacatos is a $1.00 bus ride away. So we walked out to the bus stop (2 blocks from our house in

2014) and flagged down the Vilcabamba bus.

The highway climbs out of Loja and reaches the entrance to Podocarpus National Park on the mountain pass a few minutes later. After that, the road winds its way down to Malacatos, descending steadily all the way. There are a few villages clinging to the hillsides, each home looking seriously in danger of sliding thousands of feet down the mountain during the next heavy rainstorm. Closer to Malacatos the land flattens out and the number of fancy homes increases exponentially.

Inside the city of Malacatos, however, the streets and buildings look like a pretty average Latin American town. When we hopped off the bus we could hear drums coming from the plaza a block away. We followed the noise of the drumbeat to find a parade in session. We pressed up against the crowd and stood on tippy-toes for a better look. All of the area schools seemed to be participating–students and teachers alike. Police officers held the crowd back so that the parade could make its way through on the walkway in front of the cathedral. The entire town turned out for the event; it was packed! Many people shielded their heads from the strong sun with their newspapers. Turns out they were celebrating Malacatos' 192nd anniversary of political emancipation.

After the parade I bought an ice cream cone ($0.25) and Keith and I set out to explore, walking past *panela* (unrefined sugar) factories, through a park, and up a country road that took us past an assortment of old, simple adobe homes and huge new brick homes with fancy landscaping. Once you're outside the main part of town, the sidewalks disappear and pedestrians share the roads with the vehicles, which fortunately are not too numerous. The sun and warmth felt good to me, even though we both found ourselves sweating as we hiked along.

Awhile later we returned to the central part of town to find lunch, and got splashed a few times by kids bearing water guns and water balloons. Thus refreshed, we found a restaurant and ate a typical Ecuadorian meal.

After lunch we continued our explorations up a country road on the opposite side of town. This time, instead of sugar factories, we found brick factories, steadily supplying the construction of all the fancy homes. We encountered a trail that followed a dry stream bed up the hill so we followed it until it eventually petered out into the stream bed itself. On the way back down we met a woman and her little girl, still dressed up from the parade, turning up a side trail and asked if that trail led back to the main road. She said it did, so we walked with them while she told us about her adobe house and about the nice views from the hills, and asked us a little bit about ourselves. At the road she shook our hands and continued up the hill, and we went back down into town to catch the bus back to Loja.

Malacatos makes for a great quick day trip if you feel like basking in some warmer weather for awhile! See photos and a video of our day in Malacatos on the companion website. (Access at **www.LilyAnnFouts.com/lojabonus**.)

Zamora

You can buy bus tickets to Zamora for $3 each. No matter which road you take out of Loja, there is a steep climb out of the valley and usually a long descent on the other side, all on winding roads. This road drops into *Amazonía*–the edge of the Amazon Basin. Although it's not far from Loja, Zamora is located outside of the Loja province. It's in the province of Zamora-Chinchipe. One of the first things you'll notice when you get there is how much more warm and humid it is compared to Loja. We had various vendors on this bus–some boarded while we waited at the station and others joined us en route–selling everything from candy to jewelry to "cures" for various ailments.

In Zamora we looked around for a hotel and settled with *Hotel Betania*, which was $25 per night in 2014. It's a clean and comfortable hotel with hot showers and the best rooftop view of the town's hillside attraction: a giant clock reported to be the largest in the world. For an additional $3 each, we also purchased a good breakfast on the rooftop terrace (note: if you go, be sure to request breakfast when you check in; they need to know ahead of time).

After dropping off our backpacks in the room, we set out to explore the town. Zamora sits at the confluence of the Zamora and Bombuscaro rivers. There are two main parks in town–one on each river. We walked the streets until we happened upon the first park, on the murky Zamora river. The landscaping is pretty nice, but the trash and graffiti here and there gave me an unwelcome feeling. As we strolled along we saw another foreign couple peering into the trees with their binoculars and consulting a bird guide. We eavesdropped for a bit to detect which language they spoke. American English.

We approached them and I asked them which guide they used for birdwatching, since I'd like to get a good one before coming back next time. They highly recommended *The Fieldbook of the Birds of Ecuador* by McMullan and Navarrete, so I purchased it and brought it on our second trip to Ecuador, though unfortunately I didn't have much of an opportunity to go birdwatching then (Keith is not as enthused about it as I am). If you have an iPad, you can also buy the *Birds of Ecuador* app and the *Hummingbirds of Ecuador* app. For links to these resources, visit the book's companion site. (Access at **www.LilyAnnFouts.com/lojabonus**.)

    Following the river downstream, we reached the confluence with the much cleaner Bombuscaro river and then walked up that river until we reached the other park. I spent some time following several long, fascinating trails of leaf cutter ants in what looked like an older area of the park, with lots of trees. Eventually we reached a section of the park which looked new. There was a huge pool for swimming, and funny animal slides which dropped into the pool, and other playground toys off to the side. I sensed there were big plans for this park. I could envision it becoming a tourist draw for visitors to Podocarpus once they finished all the construction and added a restaurant (for which the building had already been built, in the center of the pool, with a bridge leading to it). (Alas, when we returned to Zamora in 2017, the promising park had fallen into disrepair. "Our new mayor does not care about keeping things nice," our taxi driver explained to us. "The last mayor built the park and had many visions for what it could become, but the new mayor does not share this vision.")

    We walked back into town and sat in the plaza–its central fountain adorned with the statue of a parakeet–to people-watch for awhile.

    Something about the central square in every Latin American town draws the residents every evening. Some come for mass at the ever-present Catholic church. The kids will be dashing around on their wheeled toys and men and women will be laughing and visiting. A rainstorm drove us back to our dry hotel room, and after dark, we climbed back up to the rooftop terrace to see the giant clock all lit up with neon lights. In Zamora I didn't find much in the way of attractions other than what I find attractive about every new town I see—simply exploring it on foot and observing the people and the scenery, interacting when appropriate.

Zamora's main attraction is the Bombuscaro entrance to Podocarpus National Park, which is quite different from the Loja and Vilcabamba sides of the park. Zamora is more tropical, and a great place to observe birds, butterflies, and waterfalls. In fact, Zamora is known as "The Land of Birds and Waterfalls."

We returned to the terrace in the morning for a breakfast of fruit juice, coffee with milk, bread, and scrambled eggs.

At the *mercado* next to the bus station, we purchased some bananas, *humitas* and empanadas for a picnic lunch ($3.25 total) and began our hike up the street toward Podocarpus, six kilometers away. (If you want to save some time and energy, you can take a taxi to this trailhead for $4.)

Unlike the Loja side of Podocarpus which is high on a mountainside and often on a ridge, this side follows the powerful Bombuscaro river. The dirt road leading to Podocarpus National Park follows the river on the opposite side from the park we had visited the previous afternoon. The scenery improves with each passing kilometer and the views of the river, the forest, and the many flowers, butterflies, and birds prompted us to pull out the camera often. We came across an old foot bridge spanning the river–still sturdy but definitely deteriorating.

We crossed to the other side and saw that the trail led up into the forest. Tempting, but we came to see Podocarpus, so we returned and continued up the road. Eventually the road ends in a parking lot and everyone must continue on foot.

At the welcome center we asked the ranger about the camping and lodging options in the park. At that time, the camping area and cabins were unfinished and visitors were still obliged to lodge outside the park. When we visited in 2017, however, they were complete. The cabins are equipped with beds and mattresses which visitors may use for a nominal fee, but lodgers must bring their own bedding. Tent campers may also bring their own equipment and camp for free.

After familiarizing ourselves with the map, we set out to tackle some trails and soon encountered another birdwatching couple–a pair of ladies from New Jersey. We chatted for awhile about Ecuador while they shared their mango with us, and then one of them offered to give us a ride into town in her rental car later on if we would give her a time to meet us at the trailhead. We happily accepted–it would give us more time to explore the park.

We decided to go to the waterfall first, then continued onward to our second destination in the park: the *Mirador* (lookout).

Between the heat, humidity, and insanely steep trail, we arrived at the top drenched in sweat, but rewarded with amazing views of Podocarpus and the Zamora valley. We pulled out our lunch and had our picnic there, then descended for our last stop: the swimming hole in the river.

We didn't have enough time to swim before hiking out to catch our ride, but we explored the shoreline and marveled at the beautiful flocks of butterflies collected there, so thick in some places that they looked almost like a carpet on the ground! (In 2017 we also hiked the longer trail that follows the river until we reached the bridge, and it is well worth it!)

    Our new friend met us as promised, and offered to show us the place where they were staying; an Eco-Lodge called Copalinga. We discovered that the birdwatching couple we had met the previous day were also staying there, and that the lodge is a popular destination for birders. The dining area is set next to a bird feeding area, so that guests can watch the many species of birds as they eat breakfast each morning. Over 220 species of birds have been observed on the Eco-Lodge property.

    We met the owners–Boudewijn and Catherine from Belgium. Boudewijn told us all about his impressive project: a hydropower generator that he built himself which produces all the power at the Eco-Lodge. With alternative energy to match Keith's interests and birdwatching to match mine, plus the ability to cater to our vegetarian diet (or pretty much any other diet, upon request), we definitely plan to splurge for a couple of nights at Copalinga on a future Ecuador visit (**www.copalinga.com**). Rates vary according to accommodation type and season, but range from $26.50 to $80 per person. Breakfast is included in the rate, with the option to purchase lunch (or a packed lunch) and dinner.

    We wished we could stay longer, but with the day coming to a close we needed to go catch a bus, so our new friend/driver took us back to town and we caught a bus to Loja a few minutes later.

    We did not travel beyond Zamora either time during our stays in Ecuador, but I understand that the region is beautiful and well worth seeing. We'll check it out next time!

Saraguro
For a unique cultural experience, take the bus north to Saraguro, named after the indigenous people in the area. One of Saraguro's main attractions is a program that connects tourists with local Saraguro families, who host the tourist for 24 hours or longer and let the travelers observe how they live. We decided to give it a try, and went to the tourism office when we arrived in town. **(www.turismosaraguro.com)**

We weren't sure if we would be good candidates due to our vegetarian requirements, but the man in the office smiled and said he had a vegetarian Saraguro family that would be a great match for us! He contacted them and made the necessary arrangements, and a little while later he drove us to their home.

The Nastacuaz Cartuche family was delightful—it turns out the father of the family is actually not Saraguro himself (he has a Colombian heritage), but the mother is, and they live in a traditional way. He made beautiful wood furniture. She and her oldest daughter crafted beautiful beaded jewelry and knitted woolen items. The wool comes from their own sheep. They shear the sheep, wash and dye the wool, and spin the yarn by hand themselves. The mother of the family showed me how to spin the yarn, and let's just say I don't have the gift. She makes it look so easy!

Our hosts had a beautiful garden, full of fruit trees and many different types of fruits and vegetables and even quinoa!

The oldest son, who was eleven years old, took us for a

lovely hike to a waterfall and up a hill through his maternal grandfather's lush cattle pasture. His grandpa is a cheese maker.

I enjoyed watching the mother of the family cook our meals, which were simple but satisfying. They included the main staples of the region—*yuca* (cassava), plantains, and a special variety of corn called *choclo* that takes eight to nine months to grow and has great, fat kernels. Many of the things she cooked for us came out of their own garden. We had some great conversations with the family during our meals.

After our stay with the family we had a little time to stroll around in Saraguro before catching our bus back to Loja. It is a quiet little town with a pretty town square.

We returned to Saraguro in 2017 with our visiting family members and once again stayed with the Nastacuaz Cartuche family. They continue to work with the tourism office, but also have their own site and Facebook page where they can be contacted directly! By booking directly with the family, they can keep more of the profits and travelers get more of a discount. Find all contact information, photos, and a link to their Facebook page at **mariacartuche.wixsite.com/posada-el-bosque**.

See photos and resources from Saraguro on the companion site. (Access at **www.LilyAnnFouts.com/lojabonus**.)

Amaluza

Amaluza is still within the Loja province, but it is one of the more distant towns we visited from Loja—four hours by bus. The last portion of the trip is on roads that were still in the process of being paved when we visited in 2014 (though the highway has been finished now).

Amaluza is the last significant town before Yacuri National Park, along the border with Peru. It's basically at the end of the line before a narrow dirt road winds over the mountains through several small villages—which many of the local people there walk to on foot—and into Peru.

Yacuri National Park wasn't on my radar until I noticed a hike being advertised on the events Facebook page for Loja. It was organized by a new hiking group called *LojAventura*, which I have mentioned previously in this book. When I told other local friends that we were going to Yacuri National Park, they generally returned blank stares. I realized this must be a remote and untouched place, if even the locals were not familiar with it.

When we stepped off the bus in Amaluza, it immediately became clear by everyone's curious stares that this was not a town accustomed to seeing foreigners. Amaluza is warmer than Loja, with a climate more similar to Vilcabamba's.

Keith and I immediately decided to spend the night in Amaluza, rather than return to Loja with the rest of the group at the end of the day. A local man who was leading the day's adventure, Arcesio, led us to a hotel (*Hostal Escorial*, phone number 072653418) where we checked in and dropped off a few things. Once everyone in our large group had arrived, we hopped into the benches on the back of the trucks that served as rural buses for the region. They call them *rancheras* or *chivas*. After another couple of hours climbing the winding mountain roads, sometimes next to sheer drop-offs, and passing a couple of remote villages along the way, we reached the entrance to the park.

Live Like a Local in Loja - Lily Ann Fouts

According to the ranger, Yacuri National Park sees fewer than 1,600 visitors per year—and almost no foreigners. Consequently, this is the most untouched and remote national park I have ever visited. The park's high altitude, pristine lakes supply the whole region with fresh water. We hiked to a lake and then up to some rocky cliffs overlooking it. The park is an absolute treasure and I wished we'd had our backpacking gear with us so we could have spent a few days exploring it.

If you're interested in seeing the park, the easiest way is to take a bus to Amaluza for $6, and then hire a taxi to drive you to the park. The cost would be $40 to take you to the park, and if you would like them to wait there for you for the day, it's $60. If you could gather a group of people to go and split the cost, it could make for a nice hiking excursion.

A much cheaper option is to take another bus or *ranchera* (which one you take will depend on the season, since buses don't drive the road during rainy season) from Amaluza to Jimbura, much closer to the park, and then take a taxi from there. Buses depart from Amaluza to Jimbura every two hours. Regular buses run from May to October or November, and *rancheras* from October or November through April due to the wetter conditions.

That night, after returning to Amaluza from an amazing hike in the park, Arcesio took our group to one of his friend's homes to see a collection of archaeological artifacts that he had collected from the region. Arcesio has a few artifacts himself, and is working toward putting together a mini-museum in Amaluza for the enjoyment of all. Late that night the rest of the group returned to Loja, and Keith and I retreated to our hotel with plans to meet Arcesio (the only person in our group actually living in

Amaluza) again the next day.

The following morning, our new friend guided us on a beautiful walk to one of the most impressive waterfalls I've seen. We walked up close and stood in the spray, feeling the strong wind generated by the thundering water. If you want to go see the waterfall for yourself, it's called *Cascada la Cofradía*. To get there, catch a taxi from town to a place called *Sitio el Coco*. From there it is a 90 minute hike up the trail. Follow the stream all the way.

We passed some wild *chirimoya* (custard apple) fruit trees along the way and Arcesio picked some for us. At the end of our hike we offered to pay Arcesio a little something for his time and for the use of his car, but he wouldn't hear of it. He insisted that he was happy to show us his hometown and wanted nothing in return. We asked him if we could at least take him out for lunch, and he agreed, so we went out for a final meal together before returning to Loja.

I recently asked Arcesio if any tourism infrastructure had been set up yet for Amaluza, and he said they're working on it, but there is nothing official yet. In the mean time, you can hire Arcesio himself as a guide or he can help point you in the right direction. His phone number is 09 97 647 390 (English is limited).

Amaluza is the small, untouched town that Vilcabamba probably once was before all the foreigners started moving in. I was smitten. To see photos and videos, visit the companion site. (Access at **www.LilyAnnFouts.com/lojabonus**.)

Of course there are many other wonderful places to visit near Loja—we feel like we haven't even scratched the surface yet! But that's all part of the fun of living in

Loja. There's so much to explore in the surrounding region, I can't imagine running out of things to see and do for a long time.

CHAPTER SEVENTEEN
Let the Adventure Begin!

Hopefully you now feel a little more informed about Loja, and maybe even Ecuador and Latin America as a whole. My husband and I fell in love with the city, but it is a good match for our personalities and tastes. Others visit Loja and hate it. I hope that after reading this book, you have a good idea of whether it is a place you *could* like or if it would definitely not fit your personality.

If Loja sounds like your kind of place, you should plan

to spend some time getting to know it before making a firm commitment to live there permanently. Walk the streets, ride the buses, shop in the local markets, attend a concert. Rent a place in a local neighborhood, join in the local activities and begin making friends. If you plan to be in Loja only for a temporary period this will not matter so much, but if you're thinking of moving somewhere permanently it becomes a much more serious matter. Give it some time!

Earlier in this book I shared the story of our frustrations with finding a furnished apartment. I'd like to finish off with a story illustrating the kindness of the people of Loja.

After we had made a few friends and received a couple of invitations, we invited two of our friends from the morning workouts over to our house for breakfast. When they found out about our struggle finding a reasonably priced apartment and discovered what we were paying, they were horrified.

"That is way too much," they agreed. "You should be paying half that."

Then they began brainstorming about how we might be able to move somewhere cheaper. "My sister has an apartment in a neighborhood up on the west side of town," said one. "We could find some furniture to loan to you and maybe you could rent from her for much cheaper."

"I have a single mom friend with a furnished house who is thinking of moving back with her family and renting it out," said the other. "I can introduce you to her."

In less than five minutes they mentioned three possible places that might be arranged for us. We even went to see one of them, and it looked promising. It gave me hope and happiness to know that our friends enjoyed having us there and wanted to help us find a way to stay. Another friend repeated this sentiment near the end of our 6-week stay in 2017. "Next time you come, let me know," he said. "I will help you find a good place to live." I have a feeling that if and when we decide to find a more permanent place in Loja, we will have help from many local friends. It all takes time, patience, and developing good relationships with the locals.

I feel honored and humbled by the kindness and friendship that was shown to us, even in the short time that we had to get to know our friends in Loja. I feel like we received a lot and couldn't really adequately return all the favors we received. I have heard similar stories from other foreigners who have spent significant periods of time in Loja. I hope in the future we can stay longer and more often and deepen the friendships that we have begun.

If you're excited about Ecuador after reading this book, go and see it! It's a beautiful country with so much variety and such friendly people. If you decide to settle in for awhile, remember the basic principles in this book:

1. Learn Spanish and use it—the locals will appreciate even the fact that you are trying. Do not expect people to speak English to you in Loja.
2. Know that there will be cultural differences that lead to frustration, but try not to get too pushy or demanding—confrontation will get you nowhere.
3. Be kind, open and friendly with the locals; answer their questions and ask them questions in return. Get to know them and their families.
4. Be respectful of families and religious and cultural traditions. Follow the lead of the locals in your manners and lifestyle as much as possible (without

being inauthentic, of course—do be yourself!).
5. Take little cultural breaks if you need them—head up to Cuenca or down to Vilcabamba.
6. Explore your new town and the surrounding communities. Enjoy the wealth of culture and nature all around!

If you want to learn more about Loja, be sure to visit the companion web page to this book. Again, you can access it at **www.LilyAnnFouts.com/lojabonus**. In the companion site, I have included helpful links, resources, book corrections and updates, and stories, photos and videos from our life in Loja. I'll add useful resources as I find them! When you sign up on that site with your first name and email address, I will send you the password to access the bonus companion site. I will also send you copies of my exclusive interviews with locals and expats, plus announcements and new updates about Loja, Ecuador, and future books I write!

One of my blog readers once asked me, "Is Loja truly a hidden expat retirement gem that will continue to gain recognition? Does it have what it takes for someone like me to seriously consider it as a place to live?"

My response is that it really depends on what kind of a person you are! For someone who is interested in learning and participating in the language and culture of Ecuador, does not have very serious medical issues, enjoys going to the symphony and hiking in the mountains, Loja is a dream. If you're more of a big city person, have sensitive health issues, want to be surrounded by people of your own culture or don't have an interest in learning Spanish or attempting to communicate with the locals, Loja is not a good fit.

I have spoken with people who loved it there, as well as people who didn't care for it. Ultimately, it's a matter of personality and personal preference. I fell in love with it myself, but I have a background in the Latin American culture and Loja has the qualities I like in a place.

I do see Loja growing in popularity and believe it could become a "hot spot" for expats, but I think the expats who are attracted to Loja are the ones interested in the local culture. During our most recent visit, I could see a real effort being made by the country, the province, and the city to improve its infrastructure, attract more tourists, and provide experiences worthy of worldwide recognition, such as the new annual International Festival of Live Arts. Loja is a special place, and its charm and culture must be respected and preserved.

I applaud you for having the courage to think of moving abroad, experiencing a new culture and learning a new way of life. Many people feel too scared to even think of such a thing, and the fact that you are open will serve you well. Remember that the keys to long-term success in Latin America will include learning Spanish and being respectful and friendly, and you'll be on your way to an unforgettable experience. *Ama la vida* (love life)!

CHAPTER EIGHTEEN

Bonus: My Next Book!

Dear Reader,

Thank you again for picking up a copy of *Live Like a Local in Loja: An Expat Experience in Ecuador*. It means a lot to me that you chose my book!

If you were intrigued by my story of growing up in Latin America (from Chapter Two), you may enjoy reading my next book, too! Here are the first few pages of my next book, *Seven Years Running*, which I co-wrote with my mom, Rhoda Friend.

Are you interested in reading the rest of the book? If so, be sure to sign up for book updates, behind-the-scenes stories, and more at **www.LilyAnnFouts.com/7yr**. We're looking for a publisher right now, and we'll let you know as soon as it's available!

Happy reading!

Seven Years Running
Lily
August 23, 1993 - Albuquerque, New Mexico

Run, run, RUN! My twelve-year-old sister, Rosy and I sprinted on adrenaline, spurred on by the police we had eluded, now several blocks behind. I willed my burning legs to keep going and struggled for breath as my feet pounded past the flat-roofed houses, the sun hot on my back.

We'd been fugitives for half of Rosy's life and had planned for this moment, but hoped it would never come. Now, the day before my fourteenth birthday, I lived my worst nightmare. Glancing back, I saw two police cars parked on the cross street behind us. Not the same two we evaded minutes earlier. *How many cops are after us?*

"Can't cry," I gasped as we hurried on. In contrast with my turbulent emotions, the eerie calm of the neighborhood accentuated the sound of our footsteps echoing against the earth-toned stucco houses.

Just ten minutes earlier, I had been calm, too. I sat peacefully at my bedroom desk, working on some biology homework. The afternoon sunlight filtered through lacy curtains and fell across the pages spread out in front of me. A soft Beethoven symphony played on the old radio next to me. I expected the mailman to show up at any minute. *Will I get any cards or gifts today?*

I tried not to daydream about the upcoming party we'd been planning with my friends and boyfriend, Charlie. I'd turn fourteen the next day, but otherwise it felt like an ordinary Monday afternoon as I turned another glossy textbook page and forced myself to focus on the assignment.

A shadow darkened my desk as a man walked by my window, distracting me again. I jumped and ran for the mailbox.

Before I reached the door, I heard an aggressive knock. *That's odd*, I thought. *Maybe he has a package for me!*

I opened the door and gasped, taking a step backward. Not the mail carrier, but a huge policeman towered in the doorway. A lump formed in my throat. I forced myself to stay calm; I mustn't look too concerned. The policeman mustn't suspect anything. Maybe he wasn't even there for us.

"Is Rhoda Friend here?" the cop asked. I started to breathe faster. The prospect of being separated from Mama—something the three of us had worked for six years to prevent—made me want to cry right then. I looked at him and replied as casually as possible.

"Uh, yeah. Just a second."

I backed away from the door and ran into the dining room. Rosy and Mama looked up from Rosy's language arts textbook on the table; their faces assumed a look of deep concern. I swallowed hard. My face felt hot, and tears threatened to spill. I managed a hoarse whisper. "Police!"

Mama jumped up and made a quick motion with her head toward the back door. Rosy and I shot out the back and ran as our mother turned toward the front door to greet our visitor.

With me in the lead, we vaulted over the cinder block wall into the yard of the neighbors to our left. Looking into the street beyond the yard, I saw we had made a huge mistake. A police car sat parked in full view on the other side of the neighbor's chain link fence. I grabbed Rosy's arm and pointed.

"We can't let them see us!"

Terrified, I attempted to climb into the next neighbor's yard, but with the ground here a couple of feet lower than the ground in our own yard, the wall was too high to scale.

Oh, no. What are we going to do? I noticed a dog house against the wall leading back into our own yard. Jumping up onto the dog house roof, I scaled back up the tall cinder block fence.

"C'mon, hurry!" I urged, turning around to pull Rosy up behind me, back into our own yard.

We jumped over the wall into the other neighbor's yard behind ours, where a large dog resided. By the time the dog noticed us, we had already jumped over the gate and into the street. He barked at our retreating backs as we rounded the corner and ran up the hill.

Rhoda
August 23, 1993 - Albuquerque, NM

The back door slammed as I walked into the living room to face the police officer. A sudden gush of wetness and warmth between my legs announced that the terror had triggered my bladder. Disgusted and embarrassed, I forced myself to remain calm. *Don't think of that right now. The girls need time. Stall. Give them time to get away.*

The blond officer looked down and sized me up with sky blue eyes.

"Rhoda Friend?" he questioned. The brass name plate, which matched the buttons of his dark blue uniform, read "Swanson." A grown up Boy Scout. *Careful, Rhoda.*

I nodded, "Yes."

He began a question, but I cut him off, not wanting to

upset Grandpa or Nana, the elderly couple for whom I did in-home care. We moved to the front porch, and as we stepped out the door, I saw two more police cruisers parked outside.

The officer began again, "We've received an anonymous tip that you took your two girls from their father against a court order. Is that true?"

He used my alias, not my legal name. He is asking for information, not telling me. He doesn't know. We have to keep it that way.

I studied his handsome face, trying to judge his character.

"What are your names and birth dates?" he pressed.

"You have our names," I said, and I gave him three false birth dates. He muttered the information into his radio.

Mr. Swanson was joined by a dark-haired, good-looking cop, with a shrewd manner about him.

"Did she do it, Steve?" asked the new cop.

"Don't know yet, Jim," he answered.

Moving to my side, with a show of sympathy, Steve stopped just short of putting his arm around my shoulders in a big-brother-is-here-to-help-you gesture. "I understand the trauma you've been through, Rhoda. This has been so hard, and now it's time to let it go."

Typical good cop/bad cop routine. Keep your cool. Play along for awhile. Buy the girls some more time.

"I want you to understand something," I looked into his eyes, "I am not telling you anything, and I admit to nothing."

"You nodded, when I was talking about your taking the girls away from their father," Steve said. That soft voice was hard to resist.

"I was merely acknowledging I understood what you were saying."

Now Steve's partner jumped in, shaking my shoulder. "We'll get the truth about this," he growled. "It will go better for you if you talk with us and come clean."

"Would you please explain to me again what is going on? I'm so confused."

Steve patiently explained again.

Jim jumped in, "You'd better start talking. You're going to jail if you don't, and you won't like what will happen there."

"Now, Jim, take it easy on her. She's been through a lot." Steve defended.

"Why would you take me to jail just because of an anonymous tip?" I continued stalling.

Jim grabbed my arm, squeezing until it hurt. I tried to move, but he backed me into a wall. "You'd better talk. We're going to find out the truth anyway, and it will be bad for you if you don't talk, or if you lie. Lying to the police is serious business."

"Whoa, whoa! No rough stuff here." Steve removed Jim's hand from my arm and put his hand on my shoulder.

"Jim here has kids. Stuff like this upsets him. We just need you to tell us what the situation is so we can help you. I'm sure everything will be just fine for you. You are obviously a good mother to those girls." His mouth broadened into an understanding smile.

I strung them along as if I would crumble at any moment, buying the girls another ten minutes. I watched two officers brush past us into the house, just as another officer approached and announced, "The names are clear—there's nothing on them."

I turned to Jim and Steve. "I refuse to talk, and I will not incriminate myself."

Jim moved in. "By your silence you admit guilt."

"Sir, you don't know your law very well. I'm not a lawyer but I know that silence can never be construed as an admission of guilt."

Jim smirked, "You probably know more about the law than I do."

The officers who had entered the house moments earlier rushed onto the porch. "The girls are gone," one of them gasped. "They must have bolted out the back."

Steve looked stern. "Cuff her."

Lily
August 23, 1993 - Albuquerque, NM
Each time a car approached, my body stiffened—the muscles tensing until the car had passed, and I knew it wasn't the police. *Slap, slap, slap*...the soles of our shoes against the sidewalk broadcast our presence to the neighborhood.

After a minute or two we were alone on the street. I grabbed Rosy's arm, slowing her down.

"We have to walk," I said. "If they see two girls running they'll know who we are. They won't be so sure if we just walk and act natural." We found a narrow lane between two high brown walls and crossed through to another street.

As an experienced child fugitive, I always kept a fanny pack containing a roll of quarters and phone numbers for emergency calls. Unfortunately, this time I had left it at home. Without my pack, we felt stranded without a way of escape.

I could keep from crying, but not from thinking. There would be no birthday party now. The knock on the door had changed everything. I would never see my friends again.

Suddenly I remembered that earlier that day I had found a quarter. Thrusting my hand into my pocket, I extracted the shiny coin.

"Rosy, look! Let's find a phone."

Heading toward a gas station, Rosy and I stood a moment outside to calm down. My sister wrung her hands and glanced back and forth, searching the area for anyone who might be after us. We didn't want the people inside to get suspicious. Taking a deep breath, we tried to look nonchalant and walked up to the counter. A twenty-something cashier smiled at us with a playful twinkle in his eye.

"Hey, how's it going?" I asked, flashing an innocent smile. "Say, would you happen to have a phone book around here?"

"Sure," the nice man said, putting it on the counter in front of us. "You want to call your boyfriend?" The twinkle flashed a little brighter at the word 'boyfriend.'

"Nah, just a friend," I tried to laugh.

Rosy and I flipped through the book and found Benny's number, then Paul's. We had Eric and Monica's memorized, but knew they wouldn't be home from work yet. Tearing the corner off a free Nickel Ad paper, we jotted down the numbers with the cashier's pen. "Thanks!" we said, dashing out the door.

A young woman wearing high-waisted, form-fitting red denim jeans and loosely-tucked, baggy T-shirt reclined against the phone booth, chewing a wad of gum. She pressed the phone to her ear through the fluffy mane of strawberry blond hair, gesturing with her free hand as if she were on her living room couch chatting with a long-lost friend. We ran into the nearby restroom on the back side of the building, fearing a passing police car might recognize us, and peeked out every thirty seconds or so.

Ten minutes later she hung up, and we hurried out to make our call. I dialed the number with a quivering finger and listened.

Ring!…….Ring!…….

"Why doesn't Benny pick up?" I muttered.

Ring! Four, five, six rings. No answer.

"Come on!"

After the tenth ring, I gave up. "He's not answering." I held the handset over the receiver for a couple of seconds, reluctant to admit defeat, then hung up. The quarter clanked into the change holder.

"See if Paul's home yet," Rosy said, cracking her knuckles. With each passing moment, we were exposed to more observers. Her gaze darted up and down the busy street, searching for any sign of danger.

I poked my finger into the change holder, removed the quarter, put it back in the slot, and dialed Paul's number. The phone rang once. Twice. After the third ring, I heard Paul's voice.

"This is Paul. Please leave your name and number, and I will get back…." I glanced at Rosy.

"Machine."

I hung up. *What if the cops already know about Paul? What would I say, anyway? We have to keep moving.*

Rhoda
August 23, 1993 - Albuquerque, NM

Jim grabbed my wrists, pulling them behind my back and snapping on the cuffs. "You have the right to remain silent." He didn't read from a card or say any more. *I know there's more to my rights than that.*

Steve moved close to me. "I want you to understand that we're detaining you, okay? This is serious. The girls ran off; that's incriminating by any law. Tell us where they are so we can get this settled."

I just shook my head and smiled.

"We've been nice, but there's one coming who won't be so nice," Jim said. Grabbing my arm, he hustled me toward a police cruiser.

With my hands behind my back, I lost my balance, stumbled, and fell. The two officers lifted me off the ground, carried me to the parked cruiser and eased me into the back seat. A small stuffed pig made from patchwork cotton fabric smiled at me from its pouch hanging from the back of the driver's seat. *They do have a sense of humor.*

Slamming the door, the police ran up the street, exactly in the direction the girls would have gone. *Did they have enough time to get away?* There was no way to know.

Lily
August 23, 1993 - Albuquerque, NM

We left the gas station, and my hopes of being rescued plummeted. To avoid being seen, we walked in a flash flood canal toward the hills. Now that we were safe from the searching eyes of the police, our tears began to flow, then dried to our cheeks almost as fast as we shed them.

"Do you think they'll put Mama in jail?" Rosy asked.

"I don't know, but I sure hope she finds a way to escape," I answered.

Our thirst accentuated the cruel August heat, even as the sun dipped lower in the sky. My tongue felt dry, and my legs prickled with sweat and dirt. We passed the fancy neighborhood on the edge of the city, with its large, southwestern-style homes and elegant rock yards landscaped with desert plants. The trailhead at the base of the Sandia Mountains lay directly ahead. To the right of the trail, a small stream emerged from the rocks and melted into the sand a few yards away.

"I don't care if the water is dirty!" Rosy said. "I'm too thirsty to care, and I'm going to drink it whether it makes me sick or not."

"Me too."

The cool water revived us, and our emotions started

pouring out.

"What are we going to do?" Rosy asked. "What if Mama's been arrested?"

"I wonder if Eric and Monica would be able to take care of us," I said. "We can think about it later. Right now it's getting late, and these mountains aren't safe at night."

I turned around to look at the western sky. The sun began to set behind the city, its rays spilling over the distant mesa, and the rocks and shrubs cast long shadows across the sand.

"Why don't we stay in the cave tonight and call tomorrow?" Rosy suggested.

"I don't know." I was worried. "There are a lot of gangs and drunk people that come up here after dark. It's probably not safe. I think we should try to get a hold of Eric and Monica. Maybe we should go down to one of those houses and ask them if we can use their phone."

"What if they get suspicious?" Rosy asked. But seeing we had limited options, she agreed and we started walking back toward the homes on the edge of the dry mountain, the golden rays shining into our squinting eyes.

As we trudged down the trail, I remembered our life when we still lived up north, before Cifer, our father, took us away from Mama and turned our lives upside down. It was a different life back then, when my name was Sierra, and Rosy's name was Spring, and Mama's name was Grace. Before the custody trial, and Mississippi, and the Bishop in El Paso. Before Mexico, when we didn't speak a word of Spanish, and my only adventure there had been a day trip over to Tijuana while we visited relatives in California. It seemed a lifetime ago.

Acknowledgments

I'd like to thank my husband, Keith Fouts, for his support and encouragement throughout the time I spent writing this book. He spent much of his precious time reading my manuscript and providing helpful feedback. I appreciate you, Sweetie!

I must also thank my friends in Ecuador for their assistance as I interviewed them for various details. I would especially like to thank Diego Diaz, Arcesio Torres, Adriana Alarcón, James White, Diana Jesuroga-Cevallos, James and Paula Hansen, Ann and Ron Keffer, and the Loja Facebook communities for their wonderful help, advice and recommendations. My sincere appreciation goes to each person we met in Ecuador, who without fail was friendly and generous toward us. I look forward to seeing you all again soon!

And last but not least, I'd like to thank YOU, dear reader. Thank you for taking the time to learn about this very special part of the world, and for supporting my work. I hope you have found value in these pages.

Don't forget to sign up for the bonus material and companion website if you haven't already! There is lots more for you there! The web page, once again, is:

www.LilyAnnFouts.com/lojabonus

Made in the USA
San Bernardino, CA
16 November 2017